TALES OF TWO SPECIES

Essays on Loving and Living With Dogs

Patricia McConnell

Wenatchee, Washington U.S.A.

Tales of Two Species
Essays on Loving and Living with Dogs
Patricia McConnell

Dogwise Publishing
A Division of Direct Book Service, Inc.
403 South Mission Street, Wenatchee, Washington 98801
1-509-663-9115, 1-800-776-2665
www.dogwisepublishing.com / info@dogwisepublishing.com

Photos: Nic Berard and Amanda Jones
Graphic Design: Lindsay Peternell

The essays in this book originally appeared in the "Both Ends of the Leash" column in *The Bark* magazine. Portions of the book later appeared in *The Other End of the Leash* and *For the Love of a Dog*. Used with permission.

Limits of Liability and Disclaimer of Warranty:
The author and publisher shall not be liable in the event of incidental or consequential damages in connection with, or arising out of, the furnishing, performance, or use of the instructions and suggestions contained in this book.

Library of Congress Cataloging-in-Publication Data
McConnell, Patricia B.
Tales of two species : essays on loving and living with dogs / Patricia Mc-Connell.
p. cm.
ISBN 978-1-929242-61-0
1. Dogs--Behavior. 2. Dogs--Social aspects. 3. Human-animal relationships. 4. Dog owners. I. Title.
SF433.M34 2009
636.7--dc22
2008042897

ISBN: 978-1-929242-61-0

Printed in the U.S.A.

To Will

TABLE OF CONTENTS

ACKNOWLEDGMENTS

First and foremost, I am grateful to Claudia Kawczynska and Cameron Woo for creating a magazine that celebrates dogs, fine writing and great art. *The Bark* is a delightful addition to our culture, and I am proud to write for it. I also want to thank *The Bark's* Senior Editor, Susan Tasaki, who has been a joy to work with, and who unceasingly makes me look like a better writer than I actually am. I also want to thank Charlene and Larry Woodward at Dogwise for their unflagging support for this work. The folks at Dogwise and I began working together when they distributed a small, paper catalog of dog and cat books and I was xeroxing my notes for clients and distributing them at seminars. Since then, Dogwise has gone on to become "The Amazon of Dog Books," and has had a profound effect on the world of dogs. They have done as much as anyone in the country to help spread the word about positive reinforcement and progressive dog training, and I'm honored to have worked with them on this book. Closer to home, Denise Swedlund and Andrea Jennings of McConnell Publishing, along with our invaluable techie prince, Joe Rhodes, deserve endless accolades for their dedication and hard work. And finally, but most importantly, I thank my pack mates, Jim Billings, Willie and Lassie, who feed my soul and fill my heart every day.

INTRODUCTION

In the year 2000 I heard about a new magazine called *The Bark* that had originated as a newsletter advocating for off-leash dog parks. The editors, Claudia Kawczynska and Cameron Woo, contacted me and asked if I wanted to write a column on dog behavior. They sounded credible, the early versions of the magazine looked great (someone called it "The New Yorker of Dog Magazines"), and so, figuring I could always stop if it didn't work out, I said yes.

To say that writing columns for *The Bark* has "worked out" is like saying that Golden Retrievers express some interest in being with people, or that Border Collies might want a little something to do on occasion. In other words, writing for *The Bark* has been a joy. It has given me an opportunity to think about the behavior of dogs—not to mention that of their people—in a thoughtful and considered way that is so often discouraged in today's print media. Bullet-pointed lists are all the rage with editors nowadays—"The top ten ways to trim your dog's nails!" or "Smart Breeds and Dumb Breeds! Which is Best for You?!" Admittedly, there is value in conveying a lot of information in a concise form, and I've happily written my share of lists and bullet points for many a source, including my own website. But what a pleasure to be allowed to sit back and contemplate the behavior of the world's two most interesting species—people and dogs.

You might think that, given the close relationship we have with our dogs, whatever needed to be said about people and dogs has been written already. Certainly there are hundreds (thousands?) of books written about dogs, scores of magazines devoted to our four-legged friends, and who knows how many websites advertising plush doggie beds and organic puppy chow. And yet, so much of our relationship has yet to be explored, or even considered. Biologists are just beginning to appreciate the wealth of information that dogs can provide about the effect of genetics on behavior. Sociologists and anthropologists have much to discover about the profound connection between us, Peter Pan versions of chimpanzees and wolves that we are. Even public health officials are finally beginning to acknowledge the importance of the relationship between people and dogs. When hundreds of people lose their lives in a hurricane because they refuse to abandon their pets, surely it's time to pay attention. And even those of us who have always loved dogs have much to learn about them. Just because you love someone doesn't mean you understand them. If you have parents, a partner or children, perhaps you know what I mean. And what about our own behavior? Why do we behave the way we do around dogs? Most importantly, how can an increased understanding of the behavior of both species improve our relationships?

That's what this book is about. My scientific training was in ethology and psychology, and the best part of my life is being able to apply those perspectives to my two favorite species. Ethologists study animals in their natural environments, asking how an individual's genetics and environment combine to influence its behavior. Historically, psychologists who studied non-human animals have focused on learning and elucidated basic principles of behavior that apply to all animals, including the ones at both ends of the leash.

Speaking of "Both Ends of the Leash," that's the name of the essays as they originally appeared in *The Bark* magazine, because the "natural environment" for the two species in question—people and dogs—is at each other's side. We simply can't imagine the history of human kind, or that of dogs, without considering the biological miracle that is the bond between us. Here we are, two species who could just as well compete against one another, but instead have joined together, fellow travelers in the adventure that we call life.

No one said it better than Henry Beston in his book T*he Outermost House.*

> For the animal shall not be measured by man. In a world older and more complete than ours, they move finished and complete, gifted with the extension of the senses we have lost or never attained, living by voices we shall never hear. They are not brethren, they are not underlings: they are other nations, caught with ourselves in the net of life and time, fellow prisoners of the splendor and travail of the earth.

My dogs are lying at my feet as I write. Lassie is fourteen and half, an aging Border Collie who is still as sweet and soft as creamery butter. Willie, the young Border Collie just turned two, is staring toward the window…toward the barn and the sheep, hoping against hope that I will stop herding the keyboard and take him out for some serious work. They are friends to me in a way that no human could ever be, and I celebrate our similarities as well as our differences. This book is for them, and for a world in which our understanding of one another is as great as our love.

Part One

NEW DOGS

A DOG BY ANY OTHER NAME

The science and art of naming your dog

"His name is Baby," Helen told me as she stroked her dog's massive black head. "Baby" weighed in at about 65 pounds, was seven years old and had bitten 13 times. The last bite had been to Helen, when she tried to stop an attack on her disabled son. Needless to say, we had a lot to talk about, and one of the topics was her dog's name. Helen explained to me that Baby had always been "her baby," and that she did everything she could to make him happy. I countered, as graciously as possible, that Baby wasn't actually much of a baby anymore. Rather, he was the equivalent of a 50-year-old man living in her house rent-free, not helping with the housework, and getting full-body massages on demand. Half jokingly, half not, I suggested that Helen change the dog's name to something more fitting of his age and appropriate role within the family.

And that's when I lost her. As soon as I mentioned changing Baby's name, Helen's face snapped shut like a book. Of course, we continued to talk through the appointment, but as I drove away, I guessed I'd never hear from her again, and I didn't, even after calling her twice and leaving messages. In hindsight, I should've waited to talk about her dog's name. Names are important, so important that Vicki Hearne wrote an entire book—*Adam's Task*—about the weight of words in our relationship with dogs. What we call our dogs has meaning, and can have important consequences, both for ourselves and for our dogs.

One of the reasons that names are so important is the effect they have on us when we say them. Calling a male dog "Baby" makes it difficult to think of him as an adult dog, and makes it easy to excuse his behavior—it gives him "puppy privileges" that should've expired long ago. Labeling a Rottweiler "Brute" (as did one of my clients) does little to convince the neighborhood that your 85-pound Rottie plays well with Yorkies. Names evoke emotions in us, and those emotions influence our behavior. Since our behavior influences the behavior of our dogs and others around us, a name—all by itself—can have a surprising amount of power.

Emotions evoked by a name can have a profound effect even if you're not conscious of it. Much of our behavior is driven by the unconscious—just look at the research of psychologist John Bargh, who found that people walk more slowly if you ask them to play word games with phrases that include indicators of age (like the words "wrinkled" and "bingo"). Believe it or not, if you're named Georgia, you are more likely to move to the state of Georgia than you are to the state of Virginia, and vice versa. (To quote columnist Dave Barry, I am not making this up.) According to David Myers in the book *Social Psychology*, people's careers are also affected by their names. Geologists and geophysicists are named George more often than is statistically predictable, and if you're named Dennis or Denise, you are more likely to go into dentistry than if you're named Tom or Beverly. Amazing stuff, yes?

Reflect, then, on the impact of naming your dog "Baby" or "Brute." You say your dog's name often, and the above-quoted research suggests that the repetition will have an effect. The good news is that the effect can be good as easily as it can be bad. I love spring tulips almost as much as chocolate (okay, not quite), and naming my huge white fluff-ball of a Great Pyrenees "Tulip" was one of the best ideas I've ever had. Just saying her name, "Twooooo-lip," still makes me smile. In a joyful swirl of classical conditioning, my love for her and for tulips are intertwined in the best of ways. Surely Tulip was aware, either consciously or unconsciously, that her name, and thus she herself, made me happy—what a wonderful start to a relationship. Along those same lines, a friend of mine is considering naming her new dog "Sparkle." After losing four beloved pets in the last year, she is more than ready to add a daily dose of light and joy into her life.

Moving to the other end of the leash, your dog's name has another and more direct effect on his or her behavior. The structure of a sound—whether it consists of soft vowels or hard consonants for example—has an influence on how your dog responds. Most of us say our dogs' names because we want their attention—that is, after all, the way we use names in human communication. No matter who it is spoken to, dog or person, "Margaret" means: "Margaret, please pay attention to me at this moment. I would like to communicate with you."

Thus, it's useful to know that different types of sounds vary in their ability to get your dog's attention. If you analyze the acoustics of spoken language, you'll find that saying hard consonants, such as "k," "p" and "d," create what are called "broad-band" sounds, with lots of energy across a range of frequencies. If you were looking at a picture of the word "Kip," you'd see a vertical spike (the broad band) for the "k" and another for the "p." Those types of sounds are good at capturing your dog's attention because they stimulate more acoustic receptor neurons in the brain than do the flatter sounds made by vowels and soft consonants. (That's one of the reasons that clickers work so well—lots of broadband sounds.)

Thus, if you want your dog's attention, you're more likely to get it if she's named Kip rather than Gwen. Of course, you can train a dog to pay attention to any sound at all if you condition her well enough, so if you want to name your dog Gwen, go right ahead. However, it's useful, especially in performance events, to be aware of the effect of sound on your dog's behavior. For example, short names with lots of hard consonants are great for people working dogs in fast-action events, such as agility and herding. The value of a short name is obvious: speed (you don't want to be singing "Gwennnn-de-lynnnnn" when you've got a tenth of a second to get a response out of your dog) and focus (the consonants at either end of a name like Kip help you keep your dog's attention). Indeed, so many working Border Collies are named "Hope" and "Jed" and "Drift" that conversations about the lineage of some dogs sound like "Who's on first?" jokes. "Is your new little bitch related to Knox's Hope?" "No, she's out of McGregor's Hope, sired by Jed." "Is that Glynn-Jones's Jed?" "No, I mean the Jed owned by…." And on and on. I've joked that for every 100 handlers in the sport, there are only 20 names for dogs.

That said, I must add that there's something satisfying about a two-syllable name—"Pixie," "Tulip" and "Sparkle" all flow off the tongue in a way that just feels good. I've also wondered if, in some cases, two-syllable names can actually help get a dog's attention, in that the first syllable acts almost as a primer for the second. Perhaps the handiest names are the ones with a lot of flexibility. My forever dog's name was Luke, but his recall signal was his name said twice: "Luke Luke!" When we were working sheep and the pressure was on, I'd belt out "LUKE!" to bring his attention back to me. In quieter times, if he did something silly, I'd say, in a rising, drawn-out drawl, "Luuuuuú-cas, what are you doing?"

Luke's name brings up one more thing to think about when you're naming your dog (and yes, of course you can change a dog's name if you don't like the one she came with!). I named Luke's daughter "Lassie," not because of the acoustics of the name, but because she came to me as a dog rejected by two people who had missed her potential to be as responsive as the television star of the same name. But listen to the consequence of that choice—say the names out loud: Luke. Lassie. I gave two dogs in the same household names that start with the same sound, and as hard I tried to keep things clear, it made life a little bit more confusing for the two of them. You can see it for yourself in a DVD I made, *Feeling Outnumbered*, in which I tell all my dogs to "Wait" at the door of the car, and then release Lassie by calling her name. If you watch carefully, you can see Luke start to move forward when he hears the "L—," and then self-correct when the rest of his daughter's name comes out. Luke and Lassie were so amenable and responsive that my mistake barely mattered, but keep this in mind when you're naming a new dog. I sure will. Living with humans is confusing enough for dogs, why make it any harder?

In summary, there are several facets of a dog's name that bear consideration. It's good to be informed about all of them, but I have to admit: When push comes to shove, I'd vote every time for the name that fits my dog's personality and makes me happy to say over a name with the "proper" acoustics. It's good to be aware of all the ways a name can affect your dog's behavior, but nonetheless, a dog by any other name…will still roll in cow pies.

SOLO

What every puppy needs from the start

I kept waiting for another one. Pip had always had five puppies, and even though the newborn pup I nestled in my arms was huge, he couldn't possibly be the only one of the litter. And so I paced up and down the room. While Pip lay quietly, I stroked her belly. Pip sighed. I begged. Pip slept.

I considered this a crisis, and not because I had a long list of puppy buyers. It felt like a crisis because of the many problem dogs I've seen in my office who came from a litter of one—the dogs who growl or snap when you touch them, who become hysterical when they can't get what they want and who go after your face when you try to pick them up. We don't know with certainty that growing up as a single puppy causes serious trouble later on in some dogs, but we have reason for suspicion. Animal behaviorists seem to see a disproportionate number of single-litter pups with serious behavioral problems in our offices. Because of that, I was sick with worry about my own Solo. Would some dear, sweet family be calling me in 10 months to tell me that the puppy I'd bred had bitten their child in the face?

For a few hours that long morning I paced around the room like an expectant mother, hoping against hope for more puppies, cuddling the newborn pup to my chest, trying to decide what to do if my fears were realized. I even considered euthanizing him, given how much trouble I'd seen from single pups. (Just in case you ever find yourself in a similar circumstance, let me advise that cuddling a healthy newborn puppy against your breast while pondering euthanasia is not the road to an objective decision.) Bathed in my own maternal hormones, I did everything but lactate myself. I could no more have euthanized this new little life over something that might happen than I could have cut off my own finger.

After a few hours of pacing and worrying, the vet confirmed my fears. "Solo" was just that, the only member of a litter of one. Ignorance is bliss they say, and, at the time, I was sorry I didn't have it. I knew far too much about the importance of early development not to worry about my pup. But I'm glad of it now, because peaceful ignorance in the short term can cause serious problems in the long run, and not just for single-litter pups. Single pups are just a subset of a much larger problem: pups who grow up in the absence of a normal amount of stimulation, whether it's from their littermates, their mother or the environment around them. I'll come back to the specific case of Solo in a bit, but right now I want to talk about the issue of early development in general. It's important because, tragically, the profound effects of early experience during the first weeks of development aren't well known by most people, and millions of dogs suffer for it.

A few years ago I was asked by a television station to tour what a reporter described as a "commercial breeding facility." You and I would call it a puppy mill. It could've been worse, although that's not saying much. Each dog was housed with four others in a relatively large pen, where they could all move around and interact. But the room where the brood bitches were kept would break your heart. Every female with a litter was housed in a small hanging, wire cage, where she and her pups lived for six to seven weeks. The mothers were never let out of their tiny cages for all that time, not to stretch their legs, not to breathe real air and most important—as any mother would know—not to get away from their puppies. But the pups...oh, the pups. They were (and are) sold, hundreds of thousands a year, to pet stores, where uninformed buyers take home damaged animals who couldn't have had a worse start in life.

It's bad enough that the pups all learn to urinate and defecate where they live, and that their only toys are their own feces. That in itself can doom their owners to a life of unsuccessful house training, but it's only one of the potential problems. The most serious problem is related to a biological phenomenon that every puppy buyer needs to know about. It's simple, really: The brains of puppies aren't fully developed at birth, and what happens in the first few weeks of life affects how their adult brains are structured. Puppies (and humans for that matter) who grow up in sterile environments have brains with relatively few connections between brain cells. Puppies who grow up in enriched environments, with lots of sensory inputs, develop into adults with a veritable spider web of connections between neurons. Those connections, called "dendritic branches," are formed early in life, and affect how many brain cells are actually used later in life.

It turns out that animals with the richest tapestry of neural connections do markedly better. "Sterile-raised" animals don't cope as well with stressors, even minor ones like meeting new individuals, adapting to a new environment or solving novel problems. Puppies who begin life in two-by-three-foot metal cages aren't exactly overwhelmed with a variety of sensory inputs, and so from the word go they are disabled, shaped by forces beyond their control into individuals with structurally deficient brains. That doesn't mean that every puppy who comes out of a puppy mill or a pet store is doomed to a life of neuroses. Canine behavior is a complicated and rich phenomenon, and there are always individuals who can shine after even the grimmest of beginnings. But many can't conquer such an impoverished start, and they and their owners will suffer for it for years to come.

The tragedy of puppy mills is well known to many of us, although it continues to shock me how successful they are. What's less known is that it's not just puppies from puppy mills who suffer from a lack of sensory stimulation in early development. Our national obsession with cleanliness and our ignorance about the consequences of environmental sterility have damaged many other puppies as well. I've worked with dogs from well-known "responsible" breeders who raised their pups in pristine cleanliness, and complete and utter environmental impoverishment. I'm not saying cleanliness isn't a virtue;

it is. But an environment isn't just "clean" or "dirty," it's not a digital "yes/no" condition. There's a wide continuum between extremely dirty and surgically sterile, and in the case of healthy puppies, the Greeks were right—"everything in moderation."

Puppies who are raised in spanking-clean kennels, but who never walk on anything but cement aren't getting as good a start in life as pups who also romped on grass, gravel, carpet and pavement. Starting at three weeks of age, pups need to experience change—the feel of different textures under their feet, the sounds of television, phones, birds singing, children crying, thunder rolling. They need to meet people of all descriptions—big ones, small ones, old ones, young ones, dark ones, light ones and ones with huge floppy hats.

The lack of an enriched, variable environment is a surprisingly common problem. Most people know that dogs need to be "socialized" during their sensitive period of social development between five and 12 weeks of age. But far fewer know that puppies, long before they go to their new homes, need a complex, changing environment in their first weeks of life to develop into the "best that they can be." It always breaks my heart to meet these dogs, the ones raised in a wire-and-cement kennel with little opportunity to grow and stretch their brains, not getting what they needed when they needed it. You can help them, but you can't go back to that critical, special period in life when their brains were ready and waiting to learn to cope with change.

I don't want to oversimplify this. It's absolutely true that exposing pups to lots of new people, to romping in grassy fields at four weeks of age and taking car rides at six weeks, creates a risk of disease transmission. It's also true that you can provide too much of a good thing. Too much stimulation at an early age can backfire on you and end up harming your puppy. Most behaviorists agree that in this case, compromise is the best course of action. I'd never take a five-week-old puppy to a busy dog park, potentially full of parvovirus particles and parasites, not to mention the problem of the pup being overwhelmed by the other dogs. But I'd take him to my friend's gravel-and-grass backyard in a minute, and let him meet her sweet, vaccinated, puppy-loving Cocker Spaniel. I'd take him in the car to the drive-up window at the bank, where he can learn to love strangers because they come with doggy treats. And I took Solo up the hill at four-and-a-half weeks of age, stumbling over tall grasses, little fat legs pumping to keep up with five grown-up dogs, where he could sniff gopher holes and eat sheep poop and God only knows what else while his brain processed the richness of earth smells and bird song and meadow mouse scents.

Solo had a different kind of environmental deprivation than pups raised in sterile conditions, but like all dogs, what happened in his first weeks of life was critical to his happiness later on. I'm thankful that Solo turned out to be fine—he's the healthy, well-adjusted pet of a woman who adores him. I don't know why he's doing so well, but I do know that I tried a number of things designed to avoid the problems that I've seen in my office. Many solo puppies have had two major behavioral problems: a lack of frustration tolerance; and an aggressive response to being touched by surprise. As I thought about it while pacing the floor the morning of Solo's birth, those problems made sense. Single pups inherently develop without the constant physical stimulation of littermates, and without the frustration of competing for a turn at the milk bar.

People who raise puppies know that from day one, nursing time isn't all sweetness and light. Puppies mew and paw and scratch in an attempt to find a nipple, and as often as not, get shoved off by a pushy littermate who wants one too. But solo pups have it all to themselves. They have constant access to a veritable cornucopia of food, readily available from eight or 10 nipples—count them!—any time they want. So I hypothesized that solo pups overreact to touch because they receive so little in the early weeks of development, and that they can't handle frustration because they never experienced it while interacting with their littermates during a critical time of development.

With that in mind, I handled Solo as often as I could, touching him while he slept, nudging him over on his back while he lay on his side. I also tortured him—at least that's what it felt like. I bought a stuffed animal the size of a puppy, and five times a day I waited until he began to search for milk, and using my surrogate littermate, pushed him aside. Sometimes I'd wait until he had sealed his tongue around the nipple and he was just getting his first squirt of milk—then I'd push him off. He'd fuss and squeal, and I'd silently apologize while Pip looked up at me in quiet confusion. Solo would paw his way back, and eventually be rewarded for his stamina.

It seemed to work. Solo displays no more frustration intolerance than any other dog last I saw him, and appears to be a well-adjusted individual. He did growl at five weeks of age when I picked him up, and my heart sank with worry that my worst fears would come true. But he responded beautifully to classical counter-conditioning—I simply touched him lightly and then immediately gave him a treat, gradually working up to firmer touches, even lifting him up before he got his treat. In four more weeks he couldn't wait to be touched, and eventually I placed him with a single woman who seemed like the perfect owner. They've been best friends ever since.

Being best friends is what it's all about, and dogs need us to do what good friends do. We need to take a stand for them, to step up to the plate to educate, advocate and fight for a normal, healthy development for every little pup born. Puppy mills, and yes, some dog-loving experienced breeders, need to understand and acknowledge that the first weeks of development can mean the difference between a good life and a troubled one. So go give your dog a kiss, and then call your local pet store and ask them not to sell puppies (or kittens). Find out if there's a puppy mill in your area and start making waves. Your dog may be getting organic chicken and acupuncture, but millions of dogs in this country aren't getting their most basic needs met, and the effects are permanent. If you're like me, one of your own basic needs is to spend time with a dog to be truly happy. Right now, dogs need us too. Our dogs don't let us down very often; it'd be good if we could say the same for our own species, wouldn't it?

Pick of the Shelter

Increase your odds of a good choice

"Chewed it in half!" he said. "In HALF!" The man on the phone was explaining to me why he had returned a dog named Lassie to the Humane Society. He'd taken her home on Thursday evening, after falling in love with her pinto fur and the black spot around one eye. Now it was Friday, and he had just returned from taking her back to the shelter. "She was so sweet," he said, "but when I left her alone in my bedroom when I went to work, she peed on the carpet and chewed my belt into pieces. I HAD to take her back, I can't put up with that."

Lassie is tucked up against my feet as I write this. Lucky me, I got her two days later—a year-old Border Collie, as sweet as a Krispy Kreme doughnut with a disposition as solid as Grecian marble. There's not a dog alive who is incapable of biting, but the chance that Lassie would bite a human is microscopically small. I've had her fourteen years now, and if I ever get another dog as good as her I probably won't deserve it. She is quite simply the sweetest, most responsive and most easily trained dog I've ever handled. She's brilliant on sheep, adores screaming children and does just about everything I ask of her. I felt a little sorry for the man who brought her back, but I've gotten over it. His inability to evaluate a shelter dog got me the dog of my dreams.

Like everyone who goes to a shelter to get a dog, Lassie's potential owner had to make a decision. Based on what he could see, in the limited time that he had, he made a decision about who Lassie was and whether she could fit into his life. Like most dog lovers, he didn't know what aspects of her behavior were immutable and which ones would respond to training and conditioning. You can hardly blame him—behaviorists and trainers aren't so sure either.

The question, as important to professionals as it is to prospective owners, is how to predict a dog's behavior in one environment based on her behavior in another one. Temperament testing of shelter dogs has become a controversial issue in the dog world, and understandably so. The stakes are high and our knowledge is limited. That doesn't mean that tremendous strides haven't been made. Leaders in the field, such as Sue Sternberg and Emily Weiss, deserve our undying gratitude for their efforts to create a standardized test to evaluate the disposition of a dog in a shelter. We've come a long way, baby, but that doesn't mean we've arrived.

So what's a prospective owner to do? While we are learning more about the influence of genetics on behavior, at a shelter you don't have the luxury of meeting your prospective dog's parents. How do you decide whether or not to take that doe-eyed shelter dog home? Although I could never cover this complicated issue thoroughly in one essay, here are some thoughts to help you pick out a good match if you don't know anything about a dog's relatives.

First off, a reality check is in order. It is impossible to perfectly predict the behavior of a dog in one context when you're doing the evaluation in another. Period. End of sentence. Impossible. The dog you see at the shelter is not necessarily going to be the dog you see after he's gotten his paws on the ground at your house. A lot of people give that concept lip service, but they don't really get it. It is simply not always possible to predict how each and every dog will behave once he or she leaves the shelter, and no matter how sophisticated temperament tests become, it never will. I've seen hundreds of dogs in my office who were sugar-sweet in all but one context—whether it's the kid on the skateboard or the Sheltie across the street—and you'd never predict their aggressive behavior if you hadn't seen it happen.

Of course, there are lots of dogs who behave in ways that do predict trouble down the road, and even some dogs who behave the same way no matter where they are or what they're doing. But there are far more dogs whose behavior varies—who are, for example, stunned into silence in the shelter but bark joyfully and relentlessly once they've slept in your bedroom for a few weeks. This shouldn't be much of a surprise, since our species is the same. You don't really know someone after drinks in a fancy bar, do you?

We can't expect dogs to be complex, thinking, feeling family members on one hand and then behave like inflexible machines on the other. That's why shelter staff and prospective dog owners are wise to borrow from scientists and think about future behavior in terms of a probability statement. Good behaviorists do this all the time, because predicting a dog's behavior is like predicting the weather. The best you can do is make a statement about what is most likely to happen in the future, based on all the information you have. There are simply too many factors that influence the weather to make responsible guarantees. That's why weathermen and scientists aren't distressed that weather predictions aren't accurate every day of the year—they know that they can't be. If you habitually complain about weather predictions being inaccurate, you might want to re-examine your understanding of a probability statement.

The implications for shelters and potential adopters are simple. Shelters should adopt dogs out for probationary periods, and welcome back with open arms any that do not work out. Of course, in the ideal world, the dog has been evaluated and is going to a home that looks like a good fit in the first place, but we all need to be prepared for the equivalent of a surprise thunderstorm. It's not loving or responsible to keep a dog who is afraid of your four-year-old child, or who begins to terrorize your thirteen-year-old resident dog. And it's not good shelter management to refuse to take a dog back after it has been adopted. (Those of you in enlightened areas might be surprised to hear how common this is in some parts of the country.)

I'm not saying it's easy to take a dog back, but no one said that the right thing to do was easy, it's just right. Ideally, shelters should help by counseling adopters about which problems might be easily fixed (like chewing on a belt) and which problems might suggest the dog would be better off in another family (like growling at the children).

I can imagine at this point that some readers might think I'm discouraging them from adopting from a shelter. Far from it. I highly recommend it. The three best places to find a dog are shelters, rescue organizations and good breeders who stand by their dogs no matter what. None of these options provide guarantees, not even the best breeders, who know the dog's genetics. If a breeder tells you that he or she has been breeding for twenty years and has never had a problem puppy, you should smile sweetly and run for the hills. The probability of that happening, no matter how careful the breeding, is infinitesimally small. Breeding is a game of odds too, not a blueprint written in ink.

Once you've acknowledged that this is a game with a certain amount of chance, the trick is to get the odds on your side. You can best do that at a shelter by finding one that does temperament testing and (here's the hard part) believing what they say about the results. Evaluations at shelters may result in probability statements rather than guarantees, but that doesn't mean they should be ignored. If the meteorologist on television says it's going to be 95 degrees and humid on Saturday, I'm not going to plan to spend the day outside. If she's wrong, I'll be pleasantly surprised, but I'd have been stupid to make an inflexible plan that most likely would have turned me and my Border Collies into puddles.

Accordingly, just because a dog snarled and bit the plastic Sternbergian "Assess-a-hand" in a temperament test doesn't guarantee that he's going to bite your child, but are you going to take the risk? That'd be akin to going surfing in a hurricane, or worse, sending your child out to do so. Sure, there's a chance it might work out, but the odds are not exactly in your favor.

The best predictions will be made by a staff that has been thoroughly trained and that has had a lot of experience handling and testing dogs. To be most helpful, temperament assessments need to be done in the same place in the same way, with clear, objective measures of behavior. But I also advocate that temperament tests include a subjective category in which experienced evaluators can say something like: "I can't tell you why, but there's something about this dog that makes me nervous." Subjective impressions, if they are made by well-trained and experienced people, can be very useful. Professionals in the most rigorous of fields know that gut feelings have value and should be included with all the other data when making a decision. The key is to be crystal clear about which is which—which parts of the evaluation contain objective, quantifiable measures and which parts are based on subjective impressions.

If you are lucky enough to have a shelter with a staff that does good testing, pay attention to their results. You're the one who's most likely to be overly influenced by a cute face, they're the ones who work with dogs all day long for a living. You just might want to listen to them.

Meanwhile, long before you fall in love with some handsome charmer in the shelter, what you can be doing is deciding what kind of a dog is right for you. That's the easy part. The hard part is not throwing your carefully developed criteria out the window once confronted with some endearing fluff-ball hunkering in the corner kennel. Taking along an objective friend who is well aware of your criteria can help keep you focused. Taking along young kids can do the opposite, so you might want to make it an adults-only trip the first time you go to the shelter. Bring the kids in once you've narrowed it down to a few suitable candidates. Here are some things that your list needs to include. They may seem obvious and trite, but be aware that I mention them because they are factors that I most often see resulting in mismatches.

Exercise needs and activity levels. Many of the dogs at shelters are high-energy adolescents whose exercise needs overwhelmed their former owners. These can be great dogs for young couples who love to play outside and go hiking, and nothing but trouble for a family with four young children. You'd take this item as seriously as it deserves to be if you could sit in my office and hear, day in and day out, the legions of people who feel guilty because they know their dog isn't getting enough exercise. Ask the shelter staff to give you their best estimate of how much a particular dog needs, and be realistic about how much more time you have in your life to give a dog both mental and physical exercise. The twenty-minute leash walk that many people define as exercise is barely enough to warm up a young retriever or herding dog.

Size. Size matters in dogs, honest. Field-bred Labradors aren't just full of energy, they grow up into big, powerful dogs who can bowl over young children and elderly parents like pins in a bowling alley. However, some of the really big dogs actually need the least exercise, so don't assume you should avoid big dogs because you don't own 20 acres. Distinguish between a big dog with high activity levels (a field-bred Labrador) versus a big dog who's a couch potato (a retired racing Greyhound comes to mind).

Reactivity and arousal levels. Dogs who are reactive to sights and sounds can kick ass as performance dogs, because they listen so well and are so quick to respond. But they can be disastrous as family pets, because they listen so well and are so quick to respond. It's one thing to have a Border Collie who reacts to your slightest movement in a sheep dog trial, it's another to have one who leaps off the couch every time your six-year-old dashes through the living room. There are two reasons good temperament tests include a segment in which the dog is hyped up and excited. One is to find out what the dog does when crazed with excitement—does he start leaping at your face and biting at you? The second is to learn, once excited, how long it takes the dog to calm down. Families with young children should look for the dog who stays relatively polite even when highly aroused, and who can calm down reasonably fast.

People oriented. Most people want a dog who likes people, but often mistake rude, overly exuberant dogs as being "friendly." Leaping up and knocking you over isn't necessarily friendly, it's either a sign of high arousal, a lack of respect for personal space or perhaps just a goofy adolescent who never learned good manners. Ask the shelter staff to help you tell the difference. I myself would avoid the dog who body slams me instead of greets me, or who ignores me completely and obsessively sniffs around the room.

Looks matter in two ways. Good looks can cause you no end of trouble—just ask a marriage counselor. Guard against throwing your list of criteria out the window for the dog whose appearance overrides your ability to make an objective decision. This is another great reason to bring a friend along. She can remind you that you swore you wouldn't take home a herding dog while you get melty-kneed over the Australian Shepherd making goo-goo eyes at you from his kennel. You might be interested to know that most people prefer dogs with some white on them, and pass up the all-brown or all-black dogs. Now that you know that, look carefully, because one of those plain Janes might just be best dog you'll ever have. But ironically, looks matter in another way. Although it might sound contradictory, it never hurts to get a dog who makes your heart smile when you look at her. I think, basically, it gets down to this: Good looks can overcome some minor deficits, but can't begin to compensate for a serious mismatch.

After all my talk about probabilities and weather predictions, I'm sure you won't be surprised when I say that none of the above will guarantee that you'll get the perfect dog. But I hope it raises the odds, and that you end up with the doggy equivalent of sunshine and blue skies when you make the humane and benevolent step of adopting a dog from a shelter or a rescue group. May you all end up with Lassies, and may all the world's Lassies find homes.

ONCE IN A LIFETIME

Why all of our dogs can't be above average

"She was amazing," said Jacqueline, talking about Belle, her recently deceased dog. "Just amazing. She adored every person and dog she ever met, and she worked for six years as a therapy dog in my practice as a psychologist. Many of my clients were mentally ill and acted erratically, but Belle loved them all, no matter how unpredictable their behavior. I never worried for a second that she'd do anything to my clients but lick their faces."

You'd think this heartwarming story would make me happy, but I wasn't feeling very happy when I heard it. Jacqueline was ready for another dog, and she wanted me to help her find a puppy to take Belle's place. In Jacqueline's own words, Belle was "one a million"— and therein lay my problem.

What's the chance that any of the puppies under consideration would be able to fill Belle's paws? You guessed it—one in a million. Okay, maybe that's a bit of an exaggeration, but we all understand the meaning of the phrase. "One in a million" dogs are as hard to find as an August snowstorm in Arizona—they're the Tiger Woods of dogdom. By definition, these dogs are so special that if you are lucky enough to have had one, you have little chance of finding another. In some ways, that's so obvious it is barely worth repeating.

Obvious, that is, until someone loses their special dog and starts looking for another. It seems relatively common to acknowledge the extraordinary nature of one dog, and then set ourselves up for failure by trying to find another one equally as good. I've known people who couldn't sleep at night, worrying about which pup to select from the litter, because they absolutely had to have the perfect dog. I know the feeling myself—many of us do. The weight of making a good decision rarely hangs as heavy as it does when responsible, educated people have to decide which pup to choose: Will it be the right one? The one who is everything I've ever wanted in a dog?

I'm not saying that we shouldn't do all we can to find the best dog available—I wish more people would think this through. It's a wise guardian who knows what he or she wants and goes out looking for it. However, it's an equally wise one who accepts what he or she gets, and goes from there. The best genetics, the best breeder or shelter, and the most impressive evaluation can only provide you with a probability statement. Puppies are like the weather. You can make good predictions about what's going to happen in the future, but the system is too complicated for guarantees. There is one guarantee we can count on, though—dogs who are "one in a million" are, well...one in a million.

Perhaps this is a good time to sit back and ask ourselves what we expect of our dogs. It seems to me that it's a lot more than it used to be. A few decades ago, dogs were expected to potty outside, to avoid eating fresh-out-of-the-nest eggs for breakfast and to not bite the children. Well, actually, that last one isn't exactly true. The most common response to a minor dog bite to the hand of a child used to be "What did you do to the dog?" or, "Didn't I tell you not to bother the dog while he's eating?" Now we are barraged with reports of millions of dog bites every year as a serious health issue, even though the vast majority of those bites are less injurious than the scrapes and scratches kids get from riding their bikes or playing soccer.

Society at large seems to expect dogs to welcome visitors with perfect manners, tolerate abusive behavior from children, stay scrupulously clean inside and outside the house, and do everything we ask of them with little or no training. Perhaps part of the problem is that there are some dogs like that—and every time someone has one, it creates the expectation that they can find another. That's a heck of a burden for the next dog to carry.

There is a positive side to our rising expectations of dogs. Surely one reason we expect so much of dogs is that we are beginning to learn more about who dogs really are. Advances in science are suggesting that dogs have emotional lives and cognitive abilities more similar to our own than previously thought. Psychologists and physicians are acknowledging the value of companion dogs to our health and well-being. We've discovered that dogs can use their noses to sniff out cancer, oil leaks and endangered turtles (no kidding). As we deepen our understanding of dogs as complex, sentient creatures, it seems that our expectations of them increase as well. That's a good thing, to some extent, but surely it's not fair to expect all of our dogs to be above average.

I had a "one in a million" dog once, Cool Hand Luke, and I count myself blessed because of it. Not just because he was so special, but because my work with other dogs reminded me daily just how special he was. Luke has been gone for several years, and now I have his nephew, a two year-old Border Collie named Will. He hasn't had a stellar start. At eight weeks, he panicked in terror at the sight of another dog at the vet clinic, and in the ensuing weeks, responded to unfamiliar dogs as though they were monsters. By the time he was three months of age, it was clear that he had potential for extreme dog–dog aggression. I'm pleased to say that Will is making notable progress on this issue (as soon as I finish this essay, his best buddy is coming over to play). However, this is not the dog who will ever take Luke's place working with clients' dog-aggressive dogs.

Problem behavior with other dogs is not the sum total of Will's sorry beginning. During his first months with me, I spent much of my time on my knees, cleaning up the results of his firehose-style diarrhea. It took three months and a lot of reading, talking and vet visits, to figure out how to handle his tender gut. Right around the time we got that under control, he began herding the cat so obsessively that both the cat and I were ready to find him a "good home in the country." (Oh, darn...I live in the country.) At nine months, the day I put down another dear and beloved dog, Will badly injured his shoulder and required five weeks of "crate rest" and leash restraint. After about three weeks of having an exercise-starved Border Collie attached to me at all times, I asked my partner Jim to take the "spawn of Satan" (those were my exact words) out of my sight for a half-hour so that I could regroup.

And yet, Will adores people of all ages, sizes and shapes. He doesn't just like them, he dissolves in ecstasy every time he meets a new one. He learns tricks faster than any dog I've ever had. He's lovely to look at, as cuddly as I am and worships the ground my Great Pyrenees walks on.

Is Will ever going to be another "one in a million" dog? I doubt it. But that's okay. I love him so much it hurts anyway. I already had my "one in a million" dog, and how many can a person expect in a life-time? If you have been lucky enough to live with one of those special dogs, remember the odds of finding another, and take the pressure off yourself to win the lottery twice. Besides, didn't our mothers tell us it's not nice to be greedy?

Part Two

EMOTIONS AND COGNITION

A GLASS HALF-FULL

All emotions may not be equal, but they are equally powerful

Buster came into the office with a record, and it wasn't a pretty one. He'd bitten several times, and the bites were serious, always given when Buster was being prevented from getting something he wanted. "I know I shouldn't say this," said Buster's guardian, "but it's almost as though he was angry at me. I know anger is a human emotion, but I swear he looks just like an angry person right before he bites."

If you're looking for a conversation-starter, just ask the people you're with if they think animals have emotions such as anger, happiness and jealousy. I guarantee an interesting, if not heated, interchange. The beliefs about emotions in animals vary from "of course animals have emotions" to "of course they don't, emotions are unique to humans." What's going on here? You would think that most of us would agree about something as basic as emotions. However, beliefs about the existence of emotions in dogs and other animals run the gamut from absolutely yes to absolutely no. And these opinions are not split along "scientist" versus "non-scientist," as is often assumed—you're just as likely to hear someone down the block argue that emotions are exclusive to humans as you are to read it in an academic journal.

The fact is, we seem to be very emotional about our emotions—we often have trouble discussing them with the pure, logical thought processes we like to think we're good at. In part, this derives from our discomfort with attributing emotions to other animals, a discomfort influenced by the work of early behaviorists, particularly B.F. Skinner. Skinner was part of a movement that was attempting to make psychology a rigorous science, and he opposed inquiry into anything that could not be measured quantitatively. Since emotions are internal, subjective states, and in Skinner's time couldn't be quantified, he argued against talking about them in animals. It's important to note that he argued with equal passion against talking about emotions in people—he wasn't one to put humans and animals in separate categories. Others took his argument one step further, aligning with the beliefs of some philosophers that there was no point in studying emotions in non-human animals—because animals don't have any.

It's true that there are good reasons to be cautious about attributing emotions to animals. We're not always very good at making attributions, imagining that a puddle on the carpet means our dogs are angry with us, when they were actually just anxious, or simply not house-trained. At times, we project our own emotions onto our pets, ignoring all evidence that they may be sad because we are feeling happy (and vice versa). However, there's no logic in arguing that we should ignore emotions in animals just because we're sometimes wrong about which ones they are experiencing. Additionally, it is no longer true that we can't apply scientific rigor to the study of emotions. Recent progress in neurobiology has allowed us to do elegant research on emotions, and the evidence is overwhelming that we share much of our emotional life with animals—including our dogs.

Emotions are primitive things, centered deep inside a primitive part of the brain. This area is called the limbic system, and it is universally found in animals such as primates (including humans), dogs and mice—it's so universal that it's actually called the "mammalian brain." We know that primal emotions like fear and happiness are critical to survival. After all, emotions allow us to decide between flight or fight. Granted, a modern version of that age-old dilemma might be whether or not to criticize your boss, but it all gets down to the same thing: Emotions inform our rational brain about the best course of action. Those decisions don't have to be conscious, but they do have to be informed. People who have lost the connection between their rational cortex and their emotional centers are unable to make the simplest of decisions, such as where to file a piece of paper. It turns out that our "rational" brains are helpless without our often-demeaned emotional side—surely a satisfying and empowering fact for those of us who wear our emotions on our sleeves.

Remember this primal power if (or perhaps I should say when) someone snorts at the idea that dogs have emotions. Remind them that the basic emotions like fear, anger and a sense of well-being are primitive mechanisms designed for the survival of animals who live in complicated, changing environments. Remind them also that dogs share the same brain structures, the same neurotransmitters, the same hormones and the same external expressions of emotions that exist in people. Even love and attachment are biological processes, chemically fueled by dopamine, which leads to the rush we feel during infatuation, and oxytocin, the hormone that warms the heart and buckles the knees when we look at an eight-week old puppy. Your dog has the same set of hormones, and they work the same way inside his body as they do inside yours. Even sheep are more attentive to and protective of their lambs if they have higher levels of oxytocin, and reject their lambs aggressively when their bodies are prevented from utilizing the oxytocin coursing through their system.

Emotions may be primitive, but that doesn't mean they are simple—which is why I would never downplay the profound differences that must exist between the experience of fear or love in a human versus the same experience in a canine. An important aspect of emotions is the thought that goes along with them, and it would be absurd to argue that a human's thoughts—fueled by our outrageously expanded cortexes—are the same as a dog's. All emotions are not equal, at least, not in terms of the brain power required to experience them.

Surely the most primitive of emotions—disgust—is experienced in profoundly similar ways in both people and dogs. "Yuck" looks the same on the face of a dog as it does on the face of a human, and it's designed to keep us alive by avoiding things that could make us sick. Fear must be next in the progression of basic emotions—how could we possibly stay alive if we weren't afraid of getting hurt?

Indeed, most biologists agree that all mammals experience what are called the "basic emotions," such as disgust, fear and anger. Things get a bit more complicated when we talk about "social emotions," which include jealousy and guilt. Many highly respected scientists, whose work I greatly admire, argue that only humans can experience jealousy, a belief fueled by the concept that jealousy requires self-awareness and an understanding of the mental life of others. I don't agree—jealousy seems profoundly simple to me: "I want it, but you've got it. I hate that." It doesn't seem very complicated does it? On the other hand, guilt is an emotion I suspect we often mistakenly attribute to our dogs. Guilt requires an understanding of social moral codes, something that does seem complicated and perhaps only relevant to human interactions. And yet, how often do we imagine that our dogs feel guilty when they greet us at the doorway and behind them we see a couch chewed into pieces?

And what about anger, the emotion that began this essay? I suspect that dogs can experience something very similar to what we call anger. I'd guess that most dogs don't get angry very often, at least not compared with humans. They may not give us unconditional love every second of every day, but their docility and patient acceptance of us is still legendary.

However, at the moment, it's the shared emotion of fear that needs our attention. The archaic "you-must-achieve-dominance-over-your-dog" perspective is experiencing a resurgence, and we are encouraged to use physical force to coerce our dogs into submission. You can get individuals to obey you by scaring them, at least some of the time—just ask kidnapping victims. But these "obedient" individuals radiate fear, and are compliant not because they've been raised to be polite and well-mannered, but because they've been threatened with physical harm if they aren't.

If we share basic emotions like fear and joy with our dogs, which the most rigorous of scientific study suggests that we do, then we need to use those big, wrinkly brains of ours to find a way to relate to dogs that brings out the best of emotions, not the worst. Of course, the way we experience emotion is different than that of dogs, and those differences are important. However, what's similar is equally important, and should inform our relationships every day. I'm reminded of the "glass half empty/glass half full" aphorism. I'm convinced that the glass is half full—and I also think it's a very big glass. The liquid within it can be bitter or sweet—it's up to us.

I'm Okay, You're Okay

A gentle hand or a tasty treat doesn't reinforce fear, it reduces it

It was one in the morning, and I was wide awake. Thunderstorms had been rolling like waves over the farm all night, and this one was so loud I thought the windows might break. Lassie, my 14-year-old Border Collie, lay panting beside me. She's almost deaf, but the combination of a falling barometer, lightning flashes and the crashes of thunder were enough to send her into a panic. As we lay there together, I stroked her soft old head, thinking about the advice to avoid petting a dog who reacts to thunder. "You'll just teach them to be more fearful," according to the traditional wisdom. Only one thing: It's not true.

We've been taught for ages that trying to soothe frightened dogs just makes them worse. It seems logical, in a cut-and-dried, stimulus-and-response kind of way. Your dog hears thunder, he runs to you and you pet him. Voilà, your dog just got reinforced for running to you when it thunders, and worse, for being afraid of thunderstorms in the first place. But that's not what happens, and here's why. First, no amount of petting is going to make it worthwhile to your dog to feel panicked. Fear is no more fun for dogs than it is for people. The function of fear is to signal the body that there is danger present, and that the individual feeling fearful had better do something to make the danger, and the fear that accompanies it, go away.

Think of it this way: Imagine you're eating ice cream when someone tries to break into your house at midnight. Would the pleasure of eating ice cream "reinforce" you for being afraid, so that you'd be more afraid the next time? If anything, things would work in the reverse—you might develop an unconscious discomfort around ice cream. However, you sure as heck aren't going to be more afraid if a burglar arrives because you were eating chocolate mocha fudge the first time it happened.

There's another reason petting your thunder-phobic dog doesn't make him worse, and it couldn't hurt to take a deep breath before you read it. Research on thunder-phobic dogs suggests that petting does not decrease the level of stress in the dog receiving it.[1] If it doesn't decrease stress, how could it act as reinforcement? Before you write describing how your loving touch calms your own dog, please note that: (1) I didn't do the research; (2) my own dogs stop pacing and whining when I pet them during storms; and (3), I don't care what the research says, it makes me feel better, it doesn't hurt anything, so I do it anyway.

Studying Stress

Humor aside, it's important to be specific about what the study actually found. The authors measured the production of cortisol, a hormone related to stress. They found that cortisol levels did not decrease when the dogs were being petted by their guardians during storms. (The most important factor in decreasing cortisol was the presence of other dogs.) Interestingly, another piece of research on social bonding found that although cortisol levels decrease in people when they are interacting with dogs, cortisol does not decrease in dogs in the same context.[2] However, in both species, other hormones and neurotransmitters increased, including oxytocin, prolactin and beta-endorphin—all substances that are associated with good feelings

---

[1]Nancy Dreschel, DVM, & Douglas Granger, Ph.D. 2005. "Physiological and behavioral reactivity to stress in thunderstorm-phobic dogs and their caregivers." *Applied Animal Behaviour Science* 95:153–168.

[2]J.S.J. Odendaal & R.A. Meintjes. 2003. "Neurophysiological correlates of affiliative behaviour between humans and dogs." *The Veterinary Journal* 165:296-301.

and social bonding. So, while petting your dog during a storm may not decrease cortisol levels associated with stress, it is still possible that something good could be happening.

On the contrary, it's just not possible that petting your dog is going to make her more fearful the next time there's a storm. Warnings that you'll ruin your dog by comforting her are reminiscent of the advice from the 1930s and '40s to avoid comforting frightened children by picking them up. That perspective was tossed out long ago by psychologists, when research made it clear that having parents one can count on when life gets scary creates bold, stable children, not dependent or fearful ones.

A Classical Approach

The greatest damage that's done with outdated "don't pet the dog" advice doesn't relate to storms, but to the pitfalls of trying to explain classical counter-conditioning (CCC). CCC can be a profoundly effective way to change behavior, because it changes the emotions that drive the behavior in the first place. A typical example in applied animal behavior is having visitors throw treats to a dog who is afraid of strangers.

Understandably, many a client has asked, "But isn't giving him treats when he's barking and growling just going to make him worse? Won't he get reinforced for bad behavior?" The answer is no, not if his behavior is driven by fear. Remember, fear is no fun, and a few pieces of food, no matter how yummy, aren't going to override the brain's desire to avoid it.

Tossing treats (or toys) to a fearful dog can teach him to associate approaching strangers with something good, as long as the treat is really, really good, and the visitor is far enough away to avoid overwhelming the dog. CCC is one of the most important tools in a trainer or behaviorist's toolbox, yet it can be hard to convince people to try it. It feels like rewarding a dog for misbehaving, and in our punishment-oriented, "you've got to get dominance over your dog" society, it is tough for some people to do. But that's exactly what I did to cure another Border Collie, my Pippy Tay, when she developed a fear of storms many years ago.

Thunder Treats

Pippy and I would run outside and play ball every time a storm loomed. Pip loved ball play, and I wanted her to associate the feelings she had when fetching with a drop in barometric pressure. Once the storm rolled in, we'd go inside and I'd feed her a piece of meat every time we heard thunder, no matter how Pip was behaving. I wasn't worried about her behavior; I was focused on the emotions inside that caused the behavior.

I even put thunder on cue. "Oh boy, Pippy, you get thunder treats!" I'd say each time we heard the thunder growl. Mind you, these words would come through clenched teeth at three in the morning, but for two summers I chirped about thunder treats, pulled out the drawer beside the bed and fed Pip after each thunderclap. By the end of the summer, Pip stopped lacerating my face with panicked attempts to crawl inside my mouth to hide from the storm. She began to sleep through moderately loud storms, not even waking up to beg for treats when the thunder rolled. She came over to me when things got really loud, but with little of the panic she'd shown before.

In the interest of full disclosure, I should share that as Pip improved, I became conditioned in the other direction. I began to dislike storms, because even the quietest of them required that I stay awake long enough to hand Pip a treat after each thunderclap. And now that Pip is gone, it seems I'll have to start again with Lassie. Sigh. Maybe I should give myself a piece of chocolate every time I hand a treat to Lassie.[3]

Fear is Contagious

I'd be remiss if I didn't mention the one way you *can* make a fearful dog worse, and that's by becoming scared yourself. The emotion of fear is so compelling that it is easy to spread around. "Emotional contagion" is the ethological term used to describe the viral spread of

---

[3]CCC is one of many ways you can help a thunder-phobic dog. I've used some of the following with good success, either on their own or, in Pippy Tay's case, combined with other methods: pheromone therapy, wraps, acupuncture, acupressure, diet change and, in serious cases, medication. If your dog is afraid of storms, you'd do well to consult a behaviorist or veterinary behaviorist for assistance in choosing the method that is right for you and your dog.

fear within a group, and it's a common occurrence among social species. If you want your dog to be afraid of thunder, strangers or other dogs, just get scared yourself. If you're afraid of storms, it is entirely possible that your dog will pick up on it and become more nervous.

However, if you are scared (and who isn't sometimes?), all is not lost. You can calm things down by concentrating on your body—slowing down your breathing and your movements, changing your posture to one of confidence and relaxation, and speaking slowly and calmly (if at all). These actions have the beneficial effect of altering your own emotions as well as your dog's. The calmer you pretend to be, the calmer you'll actually feel.

I kept that in mind last night as I cooed, "Oh boy! Thunder treats!" and fed Lassie tasty snacks from the bedside table. I had a lot more reasons to be scared than she did—she didn't know that the basement was flooding, the white water crashing down the hill was threatening to take out the barn, and the roads were washing away all around us. All she knew was that every thunder roll predicted a piece of chicken, and that I seemed to think it was a great game. She settled down relatively soon, but I lay awake for hours. I guess it really is time to put some chocolate in the drawer beside the bed. If, the next time they see me, friends notice that I've gained a lot of weight, they'll know it's been a stormy summer.

Check Your Assumptions at the Door

A dog's learning capabilities

Not long ago, a philosophy professor told one of my students that animals were incapable of learning. The same day, a client told me her dog was pawing the floor around his dinner bowl because the dog knew her fastidious mother was coming to visit. My client thought her dog had learned how important a clean house was during Mum's visits, and was trying to tidy up before she arrived.

These antithetical perspectives on the learning abilities of animals reflect our collective confusion about what goes on inside the heads of our non-human best friends. It's amazing to think that we can live so closely with dogs and yet think of them as little more than automatons, or as short furry people with tails.

You might think the examples above are extreme, but I hear comments from both ends of the continuum regularly. Friends told me recently that their sister-in-law, a highly educated and articulate woman, announced at a family gathering that "animals can't learn." In response to their stunned faces, she modified her statement: "Well, except chimpanzees, of course." When my dog-loving friends continued staring at her, dumbfounded, she amended: "And, of course, some dogs."

"Some dogs." Not all dogs, just some of 'em. Good grief. I'm shocked that it's necessary to explain to anyone—even someone living in a cave eating roots and tubers—that dogs can learn. How could anyone not know that *all* animals can learn? After all, if it hadn't been for hundreds of thousands of rats and pigeons and hapless flatworms, we would never have teased out the universal principles of learning theory. Not only do animals (even single-celled specimens) learn, but the process of learning is pretty much the same whether you're a pigeon, a planarian or, come to think of it, a philosophy professor.

I'm not sure where we're failing as science educators, but the fact that animals can learn should be common knowledge. I suppose I shouldn't be surprised that it's not, however. Surveys show that Americans are sorely lacking in knowledge about animals, in spite of our love for them. A healthy percentage of Americans don't even categorize birds or insects as animals. Sigh. Perhaps if we taught a little less math and a little more ethology and psychology in science classes we'd be better off. It's not that I have anything against math—I loved algebra and calculus—but I'd rather my neighbor knew that dogs can learn (and that insects are animals) than how to solve a quadratic equation.

However, we need to guard against leaping too far to the other end of the spectrum. Just because dogs can learn doesn't mean that they have the kind of Einsteinian mental capabilities that are sometimes ascribed to them. I doubt that the most brilliant of dogs would start mopping up around the dinner bowl in anticipation of a visit from Mum, even if Mum does arrive with white gloves and a feather duster. We do dogs no favors by imagining them capable of learning at a human level. Dogs deserve to be just that, dogs. Giving them value by making them as human-like as possible isn't respectful or useful.

Scientists who do careful, controlled experiments on canine learning and problem-solving are few and far between, and they deserve our attention and support. Even in science, familiarity apparently breeds contempt—seeking funding for research on dog behavior has often been a fool's errand. There are over a thousand published papers on the songs and calls of red-winged blackbirds. Last I looked, there were twenty or so on the vocalizations of dogs. But recently, some serious attention has been paid to the behavior of the domestic dog, and studies like these will help us avoid the extremes of thinking that dogs are either robots or four-footed humans with bad bathroom habits. Here are two such studies, which I highlight to whet your appetite for more, and to encourage a thoughtful discussion about the mental life of dogs.

The first study involves an exercise called the "non-matching to sample" test. In this experiment, an animal is first taught to respond to a particular object—let's say, a wooden square. After that response is established, the animal is presented with two objects: one is the familiar wooden square and the other is a novel object, say, a plastic ball. To get the food reward, the animal must learn to respond to the new object, in this case the plastic ball. That's the "non-matching" part: You must respond to the different object to get rewarded. Chimps and children pick this up pretty fast, but dogs are amazingly slow at it. It takes them hundreds of trials to finally start choosing the object that's different from the one on which they were first trained.[1]

One interpretation of these results is that dogs just aren't as smart as primates, poor little things, and aren't able to grasp a concept as abstract as "different." But when the experiment was redone using a spatial distinction (select the right side if you were originally trained to choose the left side), rather than one related to an object, the dogs had little trouble making the correct choice. It seems dogs have no problem with the concept of "different" if it's presented in a way that's meaningful to them.

Humans show the same selective ability, efficiently solving problems only if the problems are couched in terms or symbols that are relevant to them. The reason I chose this particular experiment is because it is such a good reminder that although *how* something is learned is universal, *what* can be readily learned is a function of genetics, natural history and experience.

That's why, no matter what method you use, you can teach a dog to sit more easily than you can teach her to heel. Dogs don't need you to teach them how to sit. What we call "training a dog to sit" is

---

[1] See Stephen Budiansky's book, *The Truth About Dogs*, for more on this study.

more accurately "training a dog to sit on cue." But heel is a different story. Dogs don't go on walks together, strolling side by side at the same pace in the same direction like primates. Of course, that doesn't mean we can't teach a dog to heel—millions of people have taught their dogs to do that beautifully. If you have good timing and know how to use positive reinforcement, it's not even that hard. But no matter how good a trainer you are, you can't teach "heel" as fast as you can teach "sit," because it's not a behavior that is relevant or natural to dogs.

What *is* relevant and natural to dogs was the focus of a second study that deserves the attention of dog lovers everywhere. Scientists at Harvard and the Max-Planck Institute[2] compared the abilities of puppies, dogs, wolves and chimpanzees to use gestural cues from humans to find hidden food. Except for the young pups, all of the individuals had had years of social experience with humans. Amazingly, puppies and dogs proved to be far more adept at this than the other test subjects. If a human gazed, pointed or tapped the ground by or toward the food, the puppies and dogs performed well over the levels predicted by chance. Their performance was far better than that of wolves, who are known to have superior problem-solving abilities, and because of that, might be expected to do better than dogs (and certainly better than silly young puppies). Dogs also out-performed chimpanzees, who, by virtue of being our closest relatives, would be expected to *be* most attuned to human gestures.

We can't really call this a "learning" study, because the investigators found no evidence of learning throughout the tests. Dogs and even very young puppies seemed to come into the experiment hard-wired to pay attention to the behavior of the human in the room. Wolves and chimpanzees, even ones who had spent years interacting with people, did not. The scientists who conducted the study suggest that the process of domestication has somehow selected for a higher degree of "social-cognitive" awareness in the domestic dog. Regardless of the derivation of this unique ability, it's yet another reminder that every species sees the world through its own perceptual filter.

---

[2]Brian Hare, Michelle Brown, Christina Williamson, Michael Tomasello. 2002. "The domestication of social cognition in dogs." *Science*, Volume 28.

The more we can understand our dogs, grasp what is relevant to them and what is not, the better we can care for them, love them and create an environment in which they will thrive. Of course, we'll never completely understand our dogs, any more than we'll ever completely understand any other human being. But somehow, I think that's a good thing, that we can work toward insights into the minds of dogs, all the while acknowledging that we'll never really know what it's like to be a dog. There's a sweetness to this paradox, to the acceptance that while we have much to learn, there will also be much we'll never know.

Simplistic notions about dogs—that they are bundles of instinct and mindless response, or that they are four-footed children with tails— may be comforting to some, but for many of us, comfort is found in the murky middle. It may be confusing sometimes, this acknowledgment that dogs are much like us in some ways and very different in others. But we can be satisfied with the knowledge that it's right and good to allow dogs a complexity that is denied by simplistic thinking. How else could we give them the respect they deserve?

WALKING THE TALK

What do dogs understand and how do they understand it?

Alex, the world's most famous African Grey parrot, died September 6, 2007, and the world is a sadder place for it.

You may be wondering why an essay about dog behavior would begin with a memorial to a parrot, but there is an important connection between Alex's behavior and that of your dog. It was Alex, and his human, Irene Pepperberg, who stretched our understanding of what goes on in the minds of nonhuman animals, including the furry best friend lying at your feet.

When, in 1977, Pepperberg began teaching Alex to use words to communicate, the consensus was that animals could be taught to associate sounds with *objects* ("Go get your ball.") but not *concepts*. Concepts are abstractions that live only inside your brain. For example, try picking up a "bigger," or giving someone a "different" as a birthday present.

The argument used to be that nonhuman animals could only respond to something directly in front of them, and weren't capable of the kind of cognitive gymnastics that abstractions require. However, Pepperberg's research taught us that not only could Alex use words to label an object's shape, form and color ("Alex, pick up the blue triangle out of all the other objects on the tray."), he had little trouble grasping concepts like "different" and "bigger" ("Alex, what color is the object that is shaped differently from all the rest?").

Alex's thought processes, and the way he communicated them, went far beyond answering questions put to him during his training sessions. One day, while looking in the mirror, Alex said, "What color?" Mind you, Alex had been trained to answer questions, not ask them. When the surprised trainers answered, "grey," Alex was then able to identify other grey objects.

That wasn't the only time Alex surprised his handlers. I am still amused by a video I saw of Alex working with an impatient trainer. After several interactions, clearly frustrating for person and parrot alike, Alex belted out, in a startlingly clear Bronx accent, "Go away!" But the bird's most compelling vocalization took place when Pepperberg had to leave him alone, for the first time, at a veterinary clinic. As she walked away, Alex said in a soft and quiet voice, "I'm sorry. I love you. I'm sorry." (This knowledge has made leaving my dogs at a vet clinic a hundred times harder for me, and I pass it along to you with my own soft and quiet, "I'm sorry." Ignorance indeed can be bliss.)

When Pepperberg first began working with Alex, there were suggestions that certain other animals could understand simple concepts, but it's only been during the last 20 years that this issue has gotten the attention it deserves. We've found that many animals—including rats, pigeons and a surprising star in cognitive research, the octopus (honest)—can functionally use concepts like "different" and "bigger."

But what about our dogs? If an octopus can understand the concept "different," surely our dogs can too. Or can they? Until very recently, research on our best friends has lagged behind that on primates and laboratory rats; apparently, "familiarity breeds contempt" in science as well as in the rest of life. But dogs are finally becoming hot topics in cognitive research—check out, for example, recent issues of the *Journal of Comparative Psychology.*

Here's a little about what we've learned so far. Research confirms that dogs can also functionally use concepts like "larger" and "different." What's more, as mentioned earlier, they can also be taught the procedure, mentioned earlier, called "delayed non-matching to sample." In this experiment, the dog is presented with an object that has a piece of food underneath. He's allowed to move the object and get the food. Then, after a delay of a varying amount of time, say, 10 seconds, the dog is presented with two objects. One item is the same as before, the other is different. The "right" choice is the different object.

When researchers first conducted the study, the dogs failed miserably. After hundreds of trials, the dogs were still unable to identify the different object. In comparison, rhesus monkeys figured it out pretty quickly. But when the researchers changed the procedure and asked the dogs to choose an object in a *different* location, our best friends turned into academic stars, getting the answer right 90 percent of the time—even after waiting 20 seconds between presentations.

So, here's where musings about cognition leave the land of the research lab and settle into your living room. Of the words you use (whether they reference actions, objects or concepts), how many do you think your dog understands? The answer may be more complicated than we think. Let me illustrate with a story.

Last night, as we have for many nights, my young Border Collie, Will, and I worked on his ability to label objects with names. He is the fastest canine learner I've ever had—and that's saying something, since I've had many other dogs, seven of them Border Collies. Will learned to lie down on his side for acupuncture in less than five minutes. He learned to stretch out his foreleg on cue in less time than I can write about it. I can ask him to "Go get your toy" five minutes after he has dropped it 200 yards away and he will retrieve it. In short, he's one of those "oh-wow" dogs who make training look easy.

But when I ask him to pick out his "ring," or his "ball," he looks like a dunce. For three weeks, I've reinforced him for touching a toy after I've said its name. I started with one object at a time, saying the name "ring" or "ball" and reinforcing a correct response with treats or play. I've done that hundreds of times, and if the only toy visible is the one I ask for, he's—not surprisingly!—always right. Recently, I've been placing two objects on the floor and asking for just one of them. At first, I make the right choice easy by placing it close to him, while the "wrong" object is farther away. But as soon as Will has a real choice, his accuracy plummets and his responses become random. He enthusiastically chooses one, and then deflates when I slowly shake my head no. Over and over, he desperately tries to figure out what I want him to do. For a while, he was choosing the last location reinforced. When he realized that wasn't it, he lay with his head down on his paws.

I didn't think teaching him "ball" and "ring" would be that hard. After all, when I say, "Get your toy" he picks up an object without hesitation. As I mentioned earlier, we've known for years that dogs can use sounds to label objects (you might well have a dog who knows his ball from his tug toy). Rico, the famous European Border Collie, not only knows the names of more than 200 objects, he could also match an unfamiliar name with an unfamiliar object in a carefully controlled experiment. How could my brilliant little dog be such a slow learner?

I think Will's struggle relates to concepts. Until I began to ask him to choose one toy over the other, the sounds I made to Will had always been associated with actions: Lie down. Walk up (on sheep). Wait. Bow. Get your toy (go pick up something). It looked as though he understood that "toy" referred to his play objects—except when I experimented and said, "Go get your ___" and he immediately picked up the closest object. When I asked him to "Go get your wallaby," he hesitated a moment, and then picked up the closest toy.

Here's another example: Will has also heard me repeatedly say in a happy, animated voice, "Where's Jim?" I've enthusiastically asked that question every time our mutually favorite guy arrives at the farm. Recently, I asked "Where's Jim?" while Jim was sitting on the couch beside us. You guessed it: Will ran to the window and danced around with excitement. So what initially appeared to be an understanding of names is really an association of sounds and actions.

Naming seems like such a simple concept, yet many of us can remember the scene in the movie *Helen Keller*, when, after infinite periods of frustration, Helen finally realizes that the sign she is being taught stands for the cold water running over her hand. Another riveting story is told in the book *A Man Without Words*, by Susan Schaller. She describes a deaf man who had never been taught even the most basic communication skills bursting into tears when he first realizes that objects could be labeled, and signs could be used to converse with others about those objects.

I'm sure Will's "Helen Keller" moment will come sometime in the future, but in the interim, his struggles are a constant reminder of the ongoing challenge to understand what's going on in a dog's brain. It's important to understand which concepts dogs understand and which they don't. Keep that in mind, and think of the following questions as wonderful ways to entertain yourself and your dog through the last cold days of winter: How much of what you say does your dog understand? What could you do to try to find out? What type of everyday concepts does your dog understand? Does your dog understand that the words you use can represent both actions and objects? Can you teach your dog to distinguish "larger" from "smaller"? You may get some definitive answers, or you may generate more questions, but whatever happens, you'll keep your dog's mind (and yours) entertained and engaged until spring arrives!

HONEST AS THE DOG
IS LONG

Dogs score high on seeing
and telling it as it is

I was at the local shelter on a mission, in a hurry to meet a dog and give a speech. Cruising through the kennels, my mind wasn't on the dogs on either side of me—until I was slammed to a stop by a face that might as well have reached out and grabbed me by my shirt. Big brown eyes in a fawn-colored frame. Silky ears. A slip of pink tongue peeking out from under a moist, black nose. "Who is *she*?" I asked as I skidded to a stop. "She has such an honest face."

"She" was Lacey, a surrendered Collie cross, and her face, like Helen of Troy's, launched not a thousand ships, but a concerted rescue effort that didn't end until she had been settled into her new home. Something about her face stopped me in my tracks and generated, in an instant, a determination not just to save her, but to find her the perfect family.

It's hard to describe what it was that so affected me, but it had a lot to do with what some call an "honest" face. I often use the term myself, even though I'm hard-pressed to accurately describe it. I'm reminded of society's failed attempts to categorize good art or offensive erotica—we can't really say what it is, but we know it when we see it. The best I can do to describe a dog's "honest" face is to say that it looks relaxed, benevolent and open, like the faces of people who seem to radiate honesty and benevolence.

Ah, but there's the rub. Honest people, yes, but honest dogs? We know for a fact that people can be honest or deceitful. But whatever am I thinking to attribute the quality of "honesty" to a dog? If only some dogs are honest, then it follows that *some* dogs aren't—and dishonesty is a characteristic usually attributed only to people.

Do dogs have it in them to be deceitful? Certainly, there are good reasons to argue that they don't. Dishonesty may be rampant in our own species, but the process of lying is complicated and requires no small amount of brainpower. Say, for example, that you're in an antique store and you break a valuable vase. Knowing that the vase costs more than you can afford, you lie to the storeowner when she asks if you were the one who broke it. But look what that lie involves—an abstract understanding of the future consequences of admitting you broke the vase (If I pay for the vase, I can't pay the mortgage and then I might lose my house…), and an awareness that the storekeeper, who has a mind much like your own, can be manipulated to your advantage.

Understanding that others have their own points of view is no small accomplishment. Children don't develop this ability until they are around four years of age—ask a two-year-old to hide from Daddy and he'll cover his face with his hands. At that age, he believes that if he can't see Daddy, then Daddy can't see him. However, children over the age of four or five are beginning to realize that everyone else has a mental life much like their own, and are able to imagine the world from the perspective of others. In other words, there's *thinking* (which most, but not all, people believe that dogs can do) and then there's *thinking about thinking*, which we don't know if dogs can do or not.

In *The Truth About Dogs*, author Stephen Budiansky suggests that they can't. He's not saying that dogs don't have thoughts, but that dogs can't think about the thoughts of others. Others argue the opposite. Stanley Coren, in *How Dogs Think*, gives examples that he believes illustrate intentional deception in canids. In one of his stories, a dog takes advantage of another dog's brief absence from the room to steal the pig ear he was chewing. She then lies down on top of it and returns to chewing on her own pig ear. The second dog returns and searches for his pig ear, which remains safely squirreled away under her body. With the other dog still in the room, she finishes hers, stretches out her forepaws like a satisfied diner at a four-star restaurant, and maintains her place. Then, as soon as the second dog leaves the room, she pulls out his pig ear from under her belly and finishes it up in peace. Clever girl.

There are other examples of what looks like strategic deception in canids. In one well-documented story, a female arctic fox was being harassed mercilessly by her own young when she brought home food, and she herself was beginning to go hungry. Finally, while being swamped yet again by her voracious litter over a kill, she jerked her muzzle upward toward the distant horizon and gave the short, sharp alarm bark characteristic of her species. Her kits immediately dashed into the underground den to safety—while she stopped attending to phantom predators and ate her first good meal in days.

We have to be careful about attributing intention and mental processes to an animal we can't interview ("Excuse me, Ms. Fox, but could you tell us what you were thinking when you barked at seemingly nothing?"), but there are enough credible stories like the ones above to suggest that dogs and their cousins are capable of stretching what we call the truth. At least *some* dogs, *some* of the time. But what stands out when you look for such stories is that credible examples of dishonest dogs are rare. Dogs may be able to lie, but it doesn't appear they do it very often. Surely part of the reason we love dogs so much is that, compared to members of our own species, dogs are pillars of the truth.

The debate about what goes on in the mind of a dog will continue for decades, if not forever, but it seems clear that we are sure about a few things. We know that, in general, a dog's mind is much simpler than ours and tends to focus mostly on the present. That's undoubtedly one of the reasons that dogs are so good for us—we tend to obsess on the past and the future, and must spend years practicing meditation techniques to master what dogs do as a matter of course. We also know that dogs vary tremendously as individuals, and that some tend to be smarter about learning to associate a sound and a behavior, for example. And some seem to be better at problem solving, appearing to strategically predict how their behavior will affect others and then doing what they can to manipulate the situation to their advantage.

This suggests that the ability to be dishonest is a continuum. For better or worse, we humans are brilliant at it, while our canine companions are awkward beginners. It might be that because dogs are so bad at it, it's easy for us to imagine they can't do it at all. Perhaps if a dog were writing this essay, it would be titled "Can humans use their noses?" After all, compared to dogs, our noses are practically dysfunctional. We are so bad at using them that dogs must wonder if we are capable of smelling anything at all.

Meanwhile, Lacey, the "honest-faced" dog from the shelter, did indeed find a good home. Her new guardians can't tell you if she's an "honest dog" or not, but she *is* good and benevolent and joyful, and the adjective still seems to fit. Honest.

KNOWING WHAT
YOUR DOG KNOWS

Probing the mysteries of knowledge

"I know he knows better!" I must have heard that a thousand times. So has every dog trainer in the country. We could decorate the sky with the words "I KNOW he knows," encased in scalloped balloons like the speech of cartoon characters, floating in the air above our heads. There's just one problem—these words are trouble. Big trouble. "Knowing" is a shaky concept at best, and the word can mean so many different things that it can end up meaning nothing at all.

It's understandable that we dog owners are quick to assume that our dogs "know" better. After all, the dog who urinated on the carpet when you went to the movie has been housetrained for months. Surely he "knew" better. My Great Pyrenees, Tulip, knows perfectly well what "Come" means, but last night she stared at me as if I had morphed into an alien speaking in tongues when I asked her to come back into the house. How many obedience competitors have a dog who lept over the broad jump in every fun match in the state and then, at a big competition, trotted around it like a silly puppy? But the dog "knew" it, right?

The word "know" is a dangerous one, in part because it presumes that knowledge is all that is needed for anyone, human or dog, to do the right thing. But think of it from our own perspective. Every one of us "knows" how to obey the speed limit when we're driving. If you can drive your car out of the garage, you have the mental and physical tools necessary to lighten up on the gas pedal. Does that guarantee that you have always obeyed the speed limit? No? But you "knew" better, didn't you? Perhaps you simply weren't paying attention, as you should have, because your mind was on something else. Or maybe you were in a hurry and consciously pushed the envelope, hoping to avoid cars with pretty red lights on top of them so you wouldn't be late to an important meeting.

I'm not excusing speeding. I'm simply pointing out that "knowing" the speed limit doesn't guarantee that any one person obeys it, any more than a dog who "knows" not to pull on a leash is going to behave in a perfectly responsible manner every time she goes out on a walk. Just as you are aware of the speed limit, but have your reasons for not always obeying it, your dog may be aware of what "Heel" means, but not always perform it perfectly.

There are myriad reasons why your dog might not perform an action that she seemed to have mastered the day before. For one thing, it takes energy for any of us—human or dog—to focus our attention, especially when we're overwhelmed with other things to think about. Perhaps, on your way home from work last night, you were thinking about a tiff you had with a co-worker, and as you replayed the conversation in your head while driving, you inadvertently started to speed up. In a similar way, your dog may have broken her heel because she was thinking about the dog around the corner who growled at her last week. Your dog wasn't being disrespectful, or "disobedient," (that's another word we'd do well to drop from our vocabulary!) she just did what we all do on occasion—lost focus for a moment.

Learning how to stay focused takes practice for dogs as well as people, and part of your job as an owner is to help your dog learn how to do it. Look at tracking dogs. No one needs to teach them how to smell, they can do that brilliantly all on their own. What they learn in training is to focus on one particular scent and to follow it while ignoring everything else. Tracking dogs who are "naturals" are dogs who are easy to keep focused (and thus harder to train to come when called if they're on a scent trail!). At the other end of the continuum, some dogs seem to have brains that leap from one thing to another like crazed frogs with Attention Deficit Disorder. But most of our dogs simply need help, just as we humans do, to learn to stay focused when surrounded by distractions.

On the other hand, you or your dog may be perfectly focused, yet choose not to do what is expected because something else seems more compelling. You might be late to pick up your children, and so you push the speed-limit envelope because you're worried about them standing outside in the rain. Your dog may decide that chasing the squirrel across the street is more important than maintaining the perfect heel that she "knows" how to perform. Knowing what's expected of us isn't always enough to get us to do it, and that's as true of dogs as it is of people. Getting mad won't help anything when things don't go as planned—better to think about what motivates your dog and find a way to make it worthwhile for her to do what you want.

There's a third reason that knowing something doesn't necessarily lead to doing it, and again, our own species illustrates it as well as dogs do. You may "know" how to hit a perfect serve, but that doesn't mean you do it every time. You may "know" your speech by heart, but you still might end up standing on the stage with your mouth gaping like a goldfish and no words coming out. Being able to perform an action in one context doesn't guarantee that you can do it in another. Actors and actresses in plays know this well, when months of practice fall apart on the night of dress rehearsal just because they changed their clothes. People who compete seriously with their dogs in any performance-related activity are well aware that they have to "proof" their dogs carefully in the context in which the dogs will be expected to perform.

But even seasoned competitors have trouble generalizing from one context to another, as do the rest of us. The same obedience competitor who goes to great lengths to help her dog practice sit/stays at fun matches often doesn't know why her dog won't sit and stay at home when visitors come. Just because they practiced sit/stays in the ring doesn't mean that the dog can contain himself at the door when visitors come. To master an activity, at least some of the practice has to happen in the location of the *performance*. If generalizing from one context to another is so hard for humans, then we can't be surprised that it's hard for our dogs as well.

As if that weren't enough, there's a fourth reason why dogs who "know" what you want might not do it, and that's a lack of agreement between you and your dog about the definition of your signal. Almost thirty years ago, my first Border Collie, Drift, drove me crazy for a couple of weeks when I was teaching him his directional commands around sheep. "Come By" means go clockwise, and "Go Away" means go counterclockwise, and for weeks he had performed it perfectly. Each time I'd give the signal he'd pivot and dash in the correct direction. Good boy, Drift. I was quite proud of both of us. But suddenly, it all fell apart. I'd say "Come By," and he'd run "Go Away." I'd say "Go Away," and he'd run "Come By." I don't know who became more frustrated, me or Drift, but training sessions got less and less fun for both of us, until I finally figured out what was going on. Without realizing it, I had inadvertently trained Drift that both "Come By" and "Go Away" actually meant "Change Direction," because I had never used the same signal twice in a row. "Come By" was always followed by "Go Away," and Drift learned that each time he heard either one of those phrases, he'd be "right" if he changed direction. Good grief. You can imagine how long it took to fix that particular disaster of miscommunication—poor Drift and I struggled for months to find a way to understand one another. And all because, without realizing it, I had never given the same signal twice in a row.

It is easy to assume that we know what our dog is thinking, but that's a fool's game at best. We don't know what's in the brain of another human half the time, much less in the mind of an individual of another species. We don't even know if one person's concept of red is the same as anyone else's. Sure, the color red has a quantifiable wavelength, but that doesn't tell us how the person standing next to us perceives it. Research on differences between men and woman has found that we don't even track time similarly. "Just a minute" turns out to mean about 55 seconds to men and closer to 65 seconds to women. But we both "know" how long a minute is, right?

Granted, understanding dogs may be a lot easier than understanding a member of the opposite sex (no wonder we call dogs our best friends!) but in either case, the word "know" often doesn't lead to understanding. So think about that when you're tempted to get angry at your dog for not doing something she "knows" how to do. I know you know that she knows, but now you know that knowing doesn't get you much.

Know what I mean?

Everything in Moderation

What do dogs need from us, and how much is enough?

There's a part of the country where dog owners call the pound to help them catch their dogs. It seems that the owners can't catch the dogs once they get out of their kennels—even when the dogs are inside fences in their owners' back yards. Apparently these poor dogs have so little contact with humans (or the contact they have is so averse), that even though they may be starved for affection, they're afraid to get close to their humans. Perhaps the dogs are aware that if they do, they'll be put right back in their kennels. (Go directly to jail, do not collect $200.)

No matter where we live, we all see an occasional dog who lives a life of loneliness, his entire world contained within the box of an isolated kennel. As hostages to a mindset that sees them as little more than property, dogs like this get as much attention as the begonias at the edge of the lawn. It breaks my heart to drive by dogs who live their entire lives in an isolated kennel, and I imagine it does yours too.

The same day that I heard about shelters being called to catch dogs inside fences, I listened to a discussion about whether it was responsible to place a dog with a person who has a full-time job. One person said she'd never place a dog with someone who was gone all day, implying that it was inhumane. I remember a heavy silence after that comment, although perhaps it was just me who stopped breathing for a moment.

When I heard that, I had four dogs. Then, as now, I work full-time during a slow week, time and a half the rest, although I'm happy to say that some of that work is done from home. But not always. Until Lassie's bladder and kidneys got too old for it, I could be away from the house for eight or nine hours at a time. When I'm home, my dogs work sheep, go on long off-leash walks, eat organic chicken and veggies, and get massages every night before they curl up on their orthopedic doggie beds. So it was a bit of a shock, years ago, to hear myself being described as inhumane to dogs because I sometimes left them home alone all day.

It seems that a remarkable thing has happened in the evolution of the domestic dog. They now have lives as varied as those of humans— some of them experience lives of misery and desperation while others have lives rich with abundance and joy. This broad continuum raises an important question: What do dogs need from us, and how much is enough?

I didn't know the answer to that question when I got my first Border Collie. Drift was two years old, and before I got him he'd spent his free time tied in a stall. Each morning when I left for work, Drift would try to go out the door with me, brown eyes melting, and I would drive away consumed with angst. Each departure felt like a betrayal, so every morning I apologized profusely to him, and drove away with guilt as my only passenger.

One day I told a friend, also a dog lover, how badly I felt leaving poor Drift every day. She looked at me as if I had lost my mind, and answered, "Let me get this straight: You feel guilty because you leave Drift home all day in a safe, temperature-controlled home. He has a soft doggy bed to sleep on, it's dry, warm in winter and cool in summer. You leave him with chew toys and balls to play with, so that he can play by himself or nap on his bed, depending on his whim. You drive forty-five minutes to your job, where you work your tail off in a difficult, high-stress environment, for little money. On the way home you drive out of your way to shop for high-quality dog food, vitamin supplements, vegetables, and more toys, all for Drift. And you feel guilty? You're crazy."

Her logic was compelling. The next day, I left for work and said: "You lucky dog you, have a good time." Within days, Drift stopped mugging my heart at the door, choosing to settle down on his bed instead. Until then I hadn't realized my emotional baggage was more of a problem to Drift than my leaving ever was.

It seems to me, that for a healthy, adult dog (puppies, of course, are a different matter altogether), what matters most is what happens before and after work. After all, canines are crepuscular: their natural activity levels are highest in the early morning and evening hours. Lucky for most dog owners, that fits in with most of our work schedules. But it also means that your dog needs you when you get home from work. If you arrive home and want to start playing on the Internet, then you have the perfect home for a stuffed dog. But what if you like to kick off your shoes, take a short walk around the yard, pour a drink and then snuffle into the cozy armchair in the living room? You've got the perfect home for an elderly dog, who needs cuddles and quiet in her last years.

Maybe you're more like me—one who considers the phrase "computer games" an oxymoron and spends less time on the couch than my dogs do. I can't wait to feed them and get us all outside. The perfect evening for me involves time to leisurely do the barn chores, time for an hour-long walk with the dogs, time to practice some challenging aspect of sheep herding with a couple of Border Collies, time to teach one of the dogs a new trick, and time to brush and cuddle them on the living room rug. In other words, the perfect evening for me lasts about six hours (dreamer that I am), and with the sole exception of my strictly enforced "no-dogs-in-the-tub-during-my-lavender-bubble-bath" policy, much of that time involves actively doing something with my dogs.

The truth is, many companion dogs are bored out of their minds. It's one thing to sleep most of the day, but it's another to get little more than a ten-minute leash walk in the evening, dinner in a bowl and a few pats on the head on the way to bed. Ironically, things were different when we didn't take such good care of our dogs. I grew up in the 1950s in an Arizona suburb, and standard practice was to wake up and let the dog out even before you started the coffee. Our dog,

Fudge, trotted down the quiet suburban road, picked up her buddies one by one, and spent the day looking for garbage, escorting the kids to the school bus, chasing the garbage men and terrorizing rabbits. Safe? No. Stimulating? Yes.

Of course I'm not advocating letting our dogs run free around the neighborhood, for reasons that are so obvious as to need no explanation. I am suggesting that dogs are complex individuals who can experience either profound boredom or mental stimulation, and that we have a responsibility to give them the latter. If we're going to take over their lives, we have a responsibility to provide them with good ones. A mind is a terrible thing to waste, and that goes for dogs as well as people.

This sentiment is shared by increasing numbers of people, and in general, that's a very good thing. It's good and right that more and more people are concerned about treating dogs as the complex, sentient creatures they are. But pendulums can swing too far, and we need to be careful not to take away one of the very qualities that we admire in dogs in the first place. For example, I see a growing number of interactive toys designed to provide dogs with mental and physical exercise, and in general I think they're great. But every yin has a yang, and we need to be careful not to inadvertently take away a quality that dogs possess, and that we humans (at least we American humans) would do well to emulate.

Dogs are specialists at accepting life as it comes to them. They are veritable masters of meditation and gurus of living in the present. But this ability isn't just genetic: Look at our own species, and compare the reaction of a Masai warrior and an American cab driver, each stranded for hours by a blocked roadway. Forgive my shameless generalizing, but I'd be willing to bet some significant money on who would be sitting patiently by the road, and who'd be pacing back and forth. We Americans live in a culture of instant gratification, but we are learning increasingly that while it may lead to a faster pace, it doesn't necessarily lead to happiness.

Not long ago I had the pleasure of cruising the trade show at the Association of Pet Dog Trainers Conference. Amid the high-end, organic doggy treat samples, hooded sweatshirts, and kennel air purifiers I found a new offering: Kong Time™ is a device that delivers five Kong™ toys to your dog, the timing randomly determined by the device itself. You stuff the Kongs with edibles, load them into the dispenser, and leave knowing that your dog will be entertained while you're gone. This is a wonderful, wonderful toy for young dogs, for dogs with separation anxiety, and for the mice in my house, who would beat out the dogs by crawling inside and helping themselves.

But like anything good, it could be misused—by well-meaning people who can't bear the idea that their dog isn't being entertained during their absence. I can see Border Collies transfixed on the toy for the entire day, obsessively waiting for the next Kong to come out. I can see some dogs, the ones who've never learned frustration tolerance, getting worse rather than better.

It should be said that I have a skewed perspective. I see a lot of aggression cases in my business, and a lot of it is caused or exacerbated by dogs who have no frustration tolerance. Like young children who've never learned emotional control, these dogs throw temper tantrums when they're frustrated. Unlike children, they have knives in their mouths, and too often they end up hurting someone. My own belief, based on many years of working with aggressive dogs, as well as years prior to that working with troubled adolescents (the human kind), is that true happiness lies in a balance of intellectual and physical challenges, emotional security, and meditative acceptance.

Perhaps in one way the answer to what dogs need is simple: They all need fresh air, healthy food, kindness, patience, and love. Just as important to their happiness, they need mental and physical exercise. But we would do well to remember that with dogs, as with humans, instant gratification isn't always the way to happiness. Sometimes it's the way to impatience, a condition that's rarely known to satisfy any animal. It's an indisputable fact that dogs need far more than food and water to be happy, and that leaving a dog jailed and alone for years is abusive (and should also be viewed as criminal).

But that doesn't mean that what's best for dogs is at the opposite end of the spectrum. I don't think we should feel guilty about leaving our adult dogs home during the day, as long as we spend our at-home hours interacting with them. If you do manage to make a living and still stay home all day with your dog, maybe you could teach your dog to go to work and earn the money you need to buy both of you dinner. Personally, I'm still trying to figure out a way to send my dogs off to work, stay home myself and have money left over for a few luxuries. I always did want to take an art class.

AUTONOMY

From free-living dogs to homebodies—what's been lost, what's been gained

Huddled together, Lassie and I spent the afternoon at the university's veterinary hospital, waiting to hear the test results. Did she have a brain tumor, or not? If so, the vets gave her two to four months, max. If not, what would explain her lack of recovery from vestibular syndrome, in which the inner ear goes wacky and temporarily destroys a dog's sense of balance? Usually, dogs recover in a few weeks, but Lassie still couldn't eat unless she was hand-fed, and she couldn't walk without weaving to the right like some drunken old Border Collie on the skids.

What I most remember about that long afternoon was not just the fear, but the overwhelming sense of responsibility for a creature who was completely and totally dependent upon me. Surely everyone who loves dogs knows the burden that comes with caring for a sick animal who can't help himself, and who can't tell you what's wrong.

Our dogs' dependence isn't confined to their illnesses. The dogs who share our lives and our homes are dependent upon us in myriad ways. They don't choose whom to live with, don't catch their own food and don't even decide when and where to go to the bathroom. (Okay, okay, I know some dogs raid the cupboards and pee on the carpet, but not if we can help it.) The fact is, most of our dogs make few decisions in life. The family dogs who used to spend the day independently trotting around the neighborhood are now kept safe and sound inside our houses, waiting for us to decide when to let them out, when to go on walks and when to take them to training class. There are, of course, a multitude of benefits—both for us and for our dogs—to having dogs live in our homes and treating them like family. There is also value in objectively asking if something has been lost in the process, even while we celebrate what has been gained.

I was stimulated to think about this cost/benefit analysis while reading *Merle's Door*, a thought-provoking book by Ted Kerasote. Man and dog adopted each other when Ted was kayaking and Merle was living on his own in the wilds of Utah, and Ted makes it clear that merging their lives wasn't always easy. Merle thought chasing cattle was one of life's greatest joys. Ted thought Merle should retire from cattle ranching and settle into the sturdy doghouse he built for him. Merle learned to stop chasing cattle, but made it clear to Ted that he had no intention of trading in his independence for a bowl of dog chow. "Merle's door" is the dog door that Ted finally installed to provide both companionship and autonomy to his new best friend.

The decision to give Merle his freedom wasn't made lightly—it was made by a man who loved his dog dearly and took his responsibilities toward him seriously. However, Merle was a special dog (the words "brilliant" and "exceptionally independent" come to mind), and Ted lived in a special place that had few dangers to free-living dogs. That's not true of most of the country. Often, dogs who run free get hit by cars, fight with others dogs or get shot by angry neighbors. I would never advocate that we go back to a life in which the average family dog is let loose in the morning and called in for dinner as the daylight fades to navy blue. The safety of dogs, not to mention the safety of our neighbors, is too important for that.

And yet, we need to be aware that safety has its costs. Surely we and our dogs both pay a price for their dependence upon us. What dogs lose is clear. They lose, in varying degrees, the same thing that we lose when we lose our freedom: the ability to do what we want, when we want to do it. I don't mean the freedom to quit our jobs and move to a tropical island. Rather, I'm talking about the moment-by-moment decisions that make up the bulk of our day—stopping work to get another cup of coffee, tossing away a book that begins to bore us.

It's true that most of us have so much freedom that we have no concept of what it's like to live without it. But we can imagine. Ask newly released prisoners what is most special about getting out, and they will tell you: freedom of choice. That might translate to the ability to turn off the light at night when one feels like it, or the choice to eat a bowl of ice cream when it's not time for dessert.

Even those of us who've never been in the slammer can relate to the importance of autonomy. Remember the first time you drove away from your parents' house, or the first night you spent in your own place? Didn't you feel freer, somehow lighter, than before? Even as an adult, don't you feel differently when, for example, your houseguests leave? No matter how much we might love a visit from friends or family, there's a sense of freedom as we watch their car drive away. Now we can eat those two remaining cookies we were too embarrassed to eat at lunch, or flop on the couch and turn on some tacky television show. Ahhh.

Surely most dogs want the same thing that we do—a certain amount of autonomy, a bit of freedom to do what they want, when they want. In their case, it might be the freedom to follow an intriguing scent, or to keep playing fetch, or to avoid the dog they've hated since the day they met her. That said, what should we do with the dogs living safely in our homes and sleeping cozy in our beds? We can't let them run free all day; it is simply not an option. Many of our dogs wouldn't want to anyway—my own dogs, Lassie and Will, would have no interest in the kind of independence that Merle demanded. Some dogs may want to roam the neighborhood and hook up with other dogs, but many of them prefer our company (bless them), no matter how strange a species we may be.

What we can do is be mindful of how often our dogs have the freedom of choice. How many walks has your dog taken in which he got to decide where to go? How often does your dog get to decide when to stop sniffing? Ever let your dog choose the direction to follow at the dog park? These are good questions to ask ourselves as we exercise our dogs' minds and bodies at dog parks and agility trials.

Six weeks after that dark day at the vet school, Lassie, tumor-free and soon to be 14 years old, helped me move a group of young lambs up a steep, wooded hill. Forcing lambs up an incline in an oak/hickory forest is hard work, especially when those lambs have never before left their mothers. I wasn't sure I could get the job done at all, much less whether my old, diminished dog could help. But I let her try, because her chest swells and her eyes shine when she knows she's been useful.

Turns out the old girl, having slowly regained her strength and her balance, was up to it. To get the job done, sometimes Lassie had to follow my instructions, but as importantly, and just as often, she had to make her own decisions. When a lamb darted away, attempting an end run back to the barn, there was no time to shout out a command. By the time my brain had recorded what was happening, Lassie had already dashed to the left, stopping the lamb like a goalie at a soccer game. It was her choice, her decision. Lassie may be old, and may be dependent upon me for much of what she needs, but she still has a brain—and surely it felt good to use it.

Part Three

COMMUNICATION

Beautiful Noises

Sit! No! Lie Down! Good Dog!

It's an amazing thing to study an animal when you don't know the purpose of the noises that they make. Scientists with IQs higher than their own weight spend years trying to translate the sounds that emanate from other animals. It turns out to be exceedingly difficult to know what an individual of another species actually means when she says, "Meow," or "Caw caw," or, of course, "Woof." But if it is that hard for us humans, what of our poor dogs? Whatever is your dog to make of the noises that she or he hears coming out of your mouth?

For a while, when I was doing my Ph.D. research, I was in a situation similar to that of your dog. I needed to analyze the words and whistles that professional animal handlers give to working domestic animals. You'd think my analysis would have been easy. I was analyzing sounds from my own species for heaven's sake. I could ask the handlers what they meant. I could play the tapes over and over again. I had all the high-tech physics of acoustic analysis at my fingertips. But being clear about what the relevant part of the signal was, when the signal stopped and started, and what the signal really meant was not easy at all. As a matter of fact, it was downright difficult. I've sympathized with dogs ever since.

After all, your dog isn't listening to the same species. He's listening to an alien, who makes noises like "come" and "down" that might as well be "blech" and "pffft" for all they inherently mean to him. No wonder so many dogs would rather play with the Cocker Spaniel next door. It's hard work to be on translation duty all the time.

But you can help. Look at the signals that you and others give to your dog from the perspective of a scientist in the field. Be Jane Goodall in your own living room for a week. You don't need any high-tech equipment at this point, just an entirely new perspective on how to listen to yourself. You be the researcher, listening to an interesting animal whose vocalizations are foreign to you.

You can start anywhere—how about with the sound "down"? Whatever must our dogs think the word "down" means? We say it to our dogs to ask them to lie down, and 10 minutes later we say "down" to get them to stop jumping up on Aunt Polly. Next, it means "get off the couch." So, what would your report say? What is the definition of "down?" What exactly is it that someone wants his dog to do when he says, "Lie down?" Lie down on her belly? Stop jumping up and stand there with all four paws on the ground? Get off the couch? Of course YOU know that the word can have different meanings in different contexts, but wouldn't this make translations tough if you were starting from scratch?

Perhaps this interesting species that you're studying also mixes "down" with "lie down." Hmmmmm. If you heard "glet" and "goo glet," would you know if they meant the same thing? How about the words "pleat" and "complete?" Each contains a note that sounds the same, but aren't the meanings different?

And what about the popular use of another set of words: "Good sit?" It's very popular now for trainers to teach dog owners to ask their dogs to sit, and then praise them by saying, "Good sit." But look at those words from a non-human perspective. If "sit" means "put your butt down on the ground," and you want your dog to do that every time you say it, what could your dog make of hearing "sit" after he's already done so? I know your dog is smart, but expecting him to read your mind about when "sit" means "do something" versus when it means "don't do anything, I am referring to something that you've already done" is a bit much, even for your smart dog!

Here's a similar question for any intrepid animal behaviorist out in the field: A lot of people say "no bark" to their dogs to ask them to stop barking (or "no bite" to stop mouthing by puppies). "No bark" certainly sounds simple, because it is just two, short words. But look at it from your dog's perspective. First of all, have you taught your dog what "bark" means? After all, it's just a noise you're making, and that noise has no meaning at all until you've taught your dog what it is. Unless your dog knows what "bark" means, how could he know what you mean by "no bark"? Secondly, look at the order of the words: If you first say "no," and then "bark," wouldn't your dog start to bark again if he knew what "bark" meant?

Doesn't your dog "come" when she hears you say, "come"? (OK, maybe not, but that's another issue. The point is you want her to, right?) Although I'm sure that dogs can pick words out of a sentence, I'm not sure that they can think in reverse, the way that "no bark" demands. My pack of crackerjack Border Collies could never learn that "Luke, OK" meant that Luke, and only Luke, was released from his stay. They would all move as soon as they heard "OK." Asking a dog to understand the grammar of "no bark" is asking a lot. Why not just say "no"?

Even if you are clear and consistent with your signals, are you sure that your dog defines them the same way that you do? For example, I suspect that most dogs and owners define the simple word "sit" differently. If you're like most pet dog owners, then you taught your dog to sit by calling her to come, telling her to sit and then reinforcing her after she did. To us, "sit" is a posture. We define "sit" as a position in which the dog's hindquarters are flexed, her butt is on the ground and her forelegs are straight, front paws flat on the ground. "Sit." Simple. And it looks like your dog defines it the same way, too, because most of the time when you tell your dog to sit, I'll bet she does just that. But what does she do if she's lying down and you say, "Sit"? Unless you've specifically taught her to sit UP (which of course you can do) she probably will stay lying down. What if she's already sitting? Many dogs actually lie down if you repeat "sit" when they already are. What if you ask your dog to "sit" when she's 15 feet away from you? Most dogs will happily trot to you and sit facing you, just as she was when you first taught her to sit. My guess is that most dogs define "sit" as an action that means: Find your owner's knees (or ankles, or belly button), stand in front of him or her and go down toward the ground.

Of course you can teach your dog to "sit" without coming to you, or to sit UP rather than sit DOWN. But the point is that you have to teach it. Unless you go beyond where most dog owners go, your dog probably defines "sit" differently than you do. What other words might your dog have his or her own definition for? I'm reminded of my favorite T-shirt, complete with goofy, grinning dog on the front, "Hi! My name is NO NO Bad Dog, what's yours?"

Please don't imagine that I think that dogs can't understand many nuances of our language. Once learned, a dog can pick "walk" out of a paragraph-long sentence. We all have dogs who eventually learned the spelling of the word "ball," much less the meaning of the word "ball" itself. Dogs constantly amaze me with their ability to act as ethologists, bent on translating the vocalizations of a confusing, yet lovable species such as ourselves. But surely we owe them as much clarity as we can muster. And when they're learning, surely we can help them along by being clear, consistent and helpful in our use of words, rather than being our usual flexible and erratic selves.

All this thoughtful consideration about analyzing sounds reminds me of some of my first research as a budding ethologist. I wanted to see if the sounds that we make to get our animals to speed up and slow down are the same no matter what language we speak. I had already gathered lots of recordings of English-speaking dog and horse handlers. I traveled from Wisconsin to the racetracks of Texas in my first attempt to record professional animal handlers who spoke a language other than English. I was looking for a cross-linguistic sample of animal handlers, and wanted to see how Spanish-speaking jockeys sped up and slowed their horses. Later I would compare them with horse and dog handlers who spoke English, Basque, Chinese, Peruvian Quechua and fifteen other languages.

But right then, I needed Spanish speakers who had never learned English, and all the jockeys hanging around the old, run-down racetrack I'd found spoke both languages. "Wait for Jose," I was told, "he'll be here any day. He knows lots of trainers and jockeys who speak no English, he'll take you to them." They were right. Jose knew everyone, and everyone knew Jose, and although Jose was as perplexed as the rest of the stable about what I was there for, he agreed to take me around to trainers and jockeys who spoke only Spanish, so that I could record them working with their horses. We set out early one morning, stopping at a convenience store on his request. He returned with a six-pack of beer. Popping a Bud, he lit a joint the size of a cigar, and said, "OK, we take you to lots of guys who talk to animals, OK? Want a hit?" I declined, and felt for my Swiss Army Knife.

Jose kept his word. I must have gotten five good recordings of non-English-speaking trainers and jockeys. God only knows what Jose said to them, my halting Spanish couldn't begin to follow their conversations. They all clearly thought I was crazy, but still, they accommodated me as you would some endearing, harmless alien.

Jose and I drove back late in the afternoon. I was exhausted and relieved and happy to have gotten so many good recordings of Spanish-speaking horse handlers. Budweisers and joints aside, Jose had been a brick. All day long he had patiently sought out handlers, translated between us, helped to lug around equipment and handle fractious horses. The sun was beginning to set when Jose suggested we finish up and drive to a little lake where we could park and watch the sunset. I firmly explained how I needed to get back to catalog and organize the recordings. The predictable and universal conversation between a young, healthy male mammal and an uninterested female mammal ensued. Jose was doing his best, but he could see he was getting nowhere. Finally, in desperation he said, to the woman who had been obsessed with recording sounds all day long: "Treesha, please come to the lake with me. I will make you such beautiful noises."

Here's hoping that the noises you make to your dog are beautiful too, because they are easy to identify, easy to understand and fun to respond to. Bless their furry little hearts for putting up with us.

CAUTION!

Your dog is watching

It was twilight, and so it was hard to tell exactly what the two dark lumps on the road were. Cruising at 70 miles an hour on the Interstate, tucked between a station wagon and a semi, I was contently driving home from a herding dog trial. But as the black shapes got closer, my state of serenity shifted. They were dogs. Live dogs, at least for the moment. Straight out of a Walt Disney movie, an old Golden Retriever and an adolescent Heeler cross were trotting in and out of the highway, oblivious to the danger. Years ago I had watched a dog get hit head-on by a car. I'd give a lot to get the image out of my head. It seemed inevitable that it was going to happen again.

I pulled off the road and parked behind another truck. Friends from the trial who were driving ahead of me had also seen the dogs. We exchanged terrified looks and ran back toward the dogs. The streaming traffic was like a flooding river, we were on one side of the road and the dogs were across the lanes on the opposite bank. They looked friendly, used to people, perhaps even happy to see something with legs instead of tires. Traffic was moving fast across all four lanes. Visibility was poor. The traffic noise was deafening, there was no way the dogs could have heard us speak to them. At just the wrong time, the dogs started ambling across the road to us. We threw out our arms and ran forward to stop them. They stopped, a microsecond before a Miller Beer truck would have hit them. For a moment we stood there frozen, terrified. The responsibility of doing just the right thing, of somehow interfering in a way that saved their lives rather than ensuring their deaths, weighed like a stone in our bellies.

We "called" to them at a break in the traffic, bending over in a play bow and turning our bodies away to encourage them to come to us. Then we would turn and stop them like traffic cops when the traffic in the next lane loomed over the hill, coming so fast I was sure they'd be killed. This silent dance of life and death continued, our bodies turning back and forth, our only means of communicating through the noise of the traffic. It all seemed to happen at the speed of light, the dogs oblivious to the danger, moving forward toward us, then stopping, then backing up as we moved our own bodies to thread them through the traffic.

But that, plus a lot of good luck, was enough. Just by shifting forward with our arms out we could stop the dogs, and by shifting backward and turning away we could get them to move toward us. No leash, no collars, no control but the effect of our bodies, communicating "come" and "stop" with just the turn of the torso. I still don't understand quite how they made it. But they did. I will forever be grateful for the responsiveness of a dog to the right visual signals.

All dogs are brilliant at perceiving the slightest movement that we make, and they assume that each tiny motion has meaning. So do we humans, if you think about it. Remember that minuscule turn of the head that caught your attention when you were dating? Think about how little someone's lips have to move to change their sweet smile into a smirk. How far does an eyebrow have to rise to change the message we read from the face it's on? One-tenth of an inch? The impact of tiny movements is equally powerful in sports. We all know that minute changes in your body's position can mean the difference between an ace or a double fault in tennis, a birdie or shanking the ball into the woods in golf. But we don't automatically generalize this common knowledge to our interactions with our dogs. For the life of me, I don't know why not.

But we don't. We are often oblivious of how we're moving around our dogs. It seems to be very human to not know what we're doing with our body, unconscious of where our hands are or that we just tilted our head.

Good animal trainers become good partly because they learn an awareness of how they're moving their body while they're interacting with their animal. Until dog lovers learn this, we radiate random signals like some crazed semaphore flag while our dogs watch in confusion, their eyes rolling around in circles like cartoon dogs. I swear there are times that I can almost see smoke coming out of dog's ears, from the strain of trying to process multiple movements from their oblivious owners. Because whether we humans are aware of our bodies or not, our dogs are tuned to us like lasers. You're "talking" to your dog with your body whether you know it or not—better be careful what you're saying. Standing straight with your shoulders squared rather than slumped can make the difference in whether your dog sits or not. Shifting your weight forward or backward less than a half an inch can lure a frightened dog toward you or chase her away. Whether you breathe regularly or hold your breath can prevent a dog fight, or cause one. I saw about ten serious aggression cases every week for over 16 years, and I learned early on that a tiny movement can change a charging Cujo into a sweetheart. Or it could get me bitten.

You might recall that I'm the woman whose Ph.D. research was on how certain sounds have inherent effects on the animals who hear them. I was primed to focus on acoustics when I moved from research to applied ethology. And all my practical hands-on work has supported what I learned: if you learn to use sound correctly you can radically improve your ability to communicate with your dog. But still, primed to listen as I was, one of the first things that hit me when I started professionally training dogs and their humans was how the humans listened to the sounds that they made to their dogs, while the dogs appeared to respond preferentially to visual signals. This observation became so compelling that two undergraduate students, Susan Murray and Jon Hensersky, and I did an experiment to see if dogs paid more attention to sound or vision when learning a simple exercise. The students taught six-and-one-half-week old puppies (four each from a litter of Beagles, Cavalier King Charles Spaniels, Border Collies, Australian Shepherds, Miniature Schnauzers and Dalmatians) to "sit" to both a sound and a motion. The pups heard a soft "beep" (replicating a spoken "sit" signal, but more consistent than if we had used our voices), which came from a tiny watch held inside the trainer's hand. Simultaneously the pups saw the trainer's same hand rise in an upward sweep above the pup's head. We wanted to replicate typical training, in which most people give both a sound signal and a visual one.

Each pup got four days of training to both signals given together, but on the fifth day the trainer only presented one signal at a time. In a randomized order, the pup either saw the trainer's hand move, or heard the beep-like sit signal. We wanted to see whether one type of signal, acoustic or visual, resulted in more correct responses. And it did. Twenty-three of the 24 puppies performed better to the hand motion than to the sound, while one puppy sat equally well to either. The Border Collies and Aussies, as you might predict, were stars at visual signals, getting 37 right out of 40 possible (and only 6 out of 40 right to acoustic signals). The Dalmatian litter sat to 16 of 20 visual signals, but only 4 of the acoustic ones. The Cavalier King Charles Spaniels showed the smallest difference between visual and acoustic signals, with 18 right of 20 possible visual signals and 10 of 20 acoustic ones. Those of you with Beagles or Miniature Schnauzers will not be shocked to learn that these puppies sat, in total, for 32 of the 40 times that they saw the "sit" visual signal, and exactly zero of the 40 times that they heard the acoustic signal. That'll teach you to call your Beagle to come when she's chasing a rabbit in the woods.

I'm playing fast and loose with numbers here, because one litter can't possibly represent an entire breed. But the results are statistically significant when you look at the pups as individuals, and they complement the experience of dog trainers everywhere—while you're chatting, your dog is watching.

This difference in focus leads to a multitude of miscommunications. First of all, as I've mentioned, many of us are downright dense about the visual signals that we send to our dogs. Even if you're a professional trainer, there are probably several that you give to your dog without even being aware of it. One of my favorite exercises is to go mute for a few hours and communicate with my dogs exclusively with my body. If you're as verbal as I am, this may require duct tape. Who knows how your dogs will respond, but I'll guess that a lot of them will be quite obedient. Some of them will be downright grateful. Of course, your dog will be more obedient if you've consciously trained with visual signals, but what matters is that *you'll* learn something. I discovered that I tend to cock my head after all my dogs came running to me. Usually I am thinking about what I'll ask them to do next. Apparently it's usually "Sit," because that's what they do when I cock my head on purpose. Once I realized it, I could cock my head in the middle of a jumble of other signals, and plop, every doggy butt hit the ground. Funny that our dogs have known these gestures all along. As Brian Kilcommons, a noted dog trainer said once, "What else do they have to do all day long but watch you?" The ultimate in co-dependents, dogs have every reason to watch us obsessively. After all, their very lives depend on it. Besides, they're dogs, and that's what dogs do.

But even when we talkative primates are aware of what we're doing with our body, we're watching through a primate filter while they're tuned to the canine channel. This leads to no small number of translation troubles. Imagine that you see someone walking toward you with a smiling face and an outstretched hand. They're looking deep into your eyes. How polite. How engaging. As you get close enough to touch, you might reach out your hand to shake theirs, or wrap both arms around their neck and chest in a warm hug. Perhaps you move your face directly to theirs and kiss their cheek. The ultimate in friendliness is to look deep into their eyes, and kiss them directly on the mouth. Ummmmm. We all want someone that we feel so good about that we greet them like that, don't we? Not if you're a dog you don't. That oh-so-polite primate approach is appallingly rude in canine society. You might as well urinate on a dog's head. Of course many dogs learn to tolerate and maybe even enjoy hugs, but they don't come hard-wired to love them.

There are several signals that turn human greetings into a bad day for a dog. Besides the threat of direct eye contact and the appalling social gaffe of an outstretched paw, whatever must they think of us leaning in toward them? Even the slightest shift forward is meaningful to a dog. So is a barely perceptible lean backwards. When dogs jump up on us, we humans tend to pull away, just as you would to avoid that unwelcome hug from the guy with gold chains in the bar. But in dog language, your "withdrawal" really means "come forward." While you're speaking NO your body is yelling YES. Surely that's one of the reasons that our dogs continue to jump up on us. Dogs stop other dogs with "body blocks," moving forward toward them and taking ownership of the space before the other dog can. When I want to block a leaping dog, I'm careful to avoid leaning or stepping back. Rather, I insure that my torso (the relevant body part) moves forward, into the dog. Move forward, most dogs stop; move back, they approach closer. We humans do it in reverse. Would you try to squelch that guy at the bar by moving closer to him? I don't think so. Move forward to a friendly human and they mirror your motion. Back away and—if you're lucky—they cease and desist.

So we need to do more than become aware of our body and how we move it. We need to be aware of how dogs interpret it. And we need to never forget that if a signal is relevant, it only takes the slightest hint of it to have a powerful effect. We share that with dogs, this responsiveness to meaningful movements, and it's both a blessing and a curse in our relationship with them.

It was a blessing that dim evening on the highway. After the dogs successfully made it across the lanes of traffic, we held on to their collars like vise grips, laughing and crying in adrenaline-charged relief. I used my car phone to call the vet clinic number on their tags. The country vet, driving back on the same highway from a dairy herd crisis, drove up in less than ten minutes. The dogs were back home within the hour. Seems the young Heeler cross had seduced the elderly Golden into no-man's land. I called the owner the next day. We both cried, grieving over what might have happened, overjoyed with what really did.

The dogs are alive because we were lucky, because the goddess of dog love was looking over us and because we knew how to talk to them with our bodies. Pay attention to yours. Your dog is.

TALES OF TWO SPECIES

Bridging the communication gap

It was springtime, and Tulip was entranced. Every ounce of her hundred pounds was quivering over the dead squirrel, drinking in the smells rising from one of nature's recycling projects. Drowning in a pool of scent, Tulip must have heard me calling her to come, because she turned her head ever so briefly in my direction, and then returned to what was important in life—attaching some of this marvelous odor to her own long, white coat. Tulip treasures a good roll in a decaying animal, much like I cherish a long soak in a lavender bubble bath. How many times have I watched her, sprawled in languorous joy on her back, an expansive grin on her face, grinding the essence of dead squirrel (or cow pie, or dead fish or fox poop) into her fur?

"Tulip," I yelled again, stepping closer to her now. This time not an ear twitched. She showed no acknowledgement of my existence. My call was louder this time, because now I was getting mad, irritated at standing in the pouring rain, at being late, at the inevitable result of my huge, soggy Great Pyrenees blowing me off. In about a half an hour, I was expecting company for an elaborate dinner party. It looked like we'd be accompanied by a huge, wet dog who smelled like old death. But she didn't roll in the squishy mess under her, because I came to my senses and stopped being just a human and started being an animal trainer. "No," I said, this time quietly, but with a pitch as low as the ground. Tulip stopped her sniffing and turned her huge, square head to look straight at me. "Tulip, come!" The "come" came out like a cheery greeting to a neighbor you'd ask over for coffee. With a brief look at the treasure below her, Tulip turned like a dancer and ran to me. I responded with a chase to the house, and let my poor, long-suffering floors get muddy yet one more time, while we tore to the refrigerator for Tulip's favorite cheese.

Tulip had done exactly what I had asked from the beginning. "Tulip," I had said at first, meaning "come," but simply saying her name and expecting her, human that I am, to read my mind about what I wanted her to do. She had acknowledged my presence politely, expressed some doggy version of "Hi Trisha, look what I found! It's a dead squirrel and IT HAS MAGGOTS IN IT!" and returned to what she'd been doing when I interrupted her. (Ever said, "Just a minute!" when someone called your name?) My saying her name again had given her no more information than before. But when I clearly communicated what I wanted, she did exactly what I asked. Tulip has learned that "no" means: "Don't do what you're doing;" and "Tulip, come" means: "I want you to stop what you're doing and come here right now." She did, as soon as I got my act together and told her what I wanted. I'm a professional dog trainer. My dissertation was on acoustic communication between professional animal handlers and their working animals. You'd think I'd have this down by now. But there's a catch. I'm a human.

Dog training is not just about dogs. It's also about humans. Most professional dog trainers spend more of their time training dog owners than they do dogs. Hang around after dog training class one night and listen to the instructors. You'll hear about that sweet little English Cocker and that dubious Labrador cross, but mostly you'll hear about Bob, Martha and Elizabeth. I won't belabor what gets said about Bob, Martha and Elizabeth—professional courtesy and all—but let's just say that it can be a tad frustrating training people to train their dogs. Beyond the statement, "Most dogs have four paws," there's only one thing I can imagine a large group of dog trainers agreeing on: Humans are harder to train than dogs.

Why might that be? Our tendency to repeat ourselves nonsensically, to get loud for no reason and to have little awareness of our body language doesn't help our dogs understand us, but we seem to keep doing it anyway. Perhaps you agree with my friend, who in answer to my question of why we behave the way we do said: "Give it up, Trisha, we're just idiots." That's one answer, with its own panache of compelling simplicity. But I like humans. I like humans as much as I like dogs. We can be brilliant, generous, joyful and endlessly amusing. But we are not blank slates who come to dog training without baggage. We are animals too, and our biological suitcases can't be left behind at the train station. Both dogs and dog lovers have been shaped by our separate evolutionary backgrounds, and what each of us brings to the relationship starts with our evolutionary heritage. Although our similarities create a bond that's remarkable, we are each speaking our own native "language." A lot gets lost in the translation. Just as we've learned a great deal about dogs from studying their progenitors, the wolves, we have much to gain by looking at ourselves as the touchy, playful and drama-loving primates that we are.

Look at what I originally communicated to Tulip: First, I said her name and she responded exactly as you might if someone said your name right now while you're busy reading this book. A brief look up, perhaps a quick comment ("Just a minute, I'm almost done reading this …"). Who knows what Tulip "said" in dog signals to me when she returned her attention to the more interesting alternative. Tulip didn't do anything wrong. Her response was socially quite reasonable. But we dog owners consistently say our dogs' names as a substitute for what we want them to do, assuming then that they can read our minds about what we really want. We don't just do this with our dogs—ask any marriage counselor how good most couples are at telling each other what they want. Just like dogs tend to chew and are mouthy as puppies, we humans tend to say a dog's name instead of telling our dog what we want.

Add on our very primate-like tendency to repeat ourselves, and its' a miracle that dogs put up with us at all. Most dog training books advise us never to repeat a command, yet every dog owner does it, no matter how good a trainer she is. Great trainers just do it less often. We shouldn't be surprised—listen to a troop of chimpanzees and you'll hear a string of notes that sound like: "Who." "Who Who." "Who Who WHO WHO WHO." When many species of animals get aroused, they start to repeat the same note over and over again, and we are no exception.

But saying it again isn't enough. Research in linguistics found that when talking to someone who doesn't understand what we say, we humans tend to repeat exactly what we said the first time, but louder. Not surprisingly, an undergraduate student, Susan Murray, and I found that humans do the same thing to dogs. A "sit" command that's ignored by the dog results in "sit" said again, but louder. We behave as if amplitude itself could somehow create the energy we need to stimulate our dogs to do something. Is there anyone in the world who hasn't, just once, yelled at his dog to "SHUT UP?" The irony of this usually escapes us during the heat of the moment: Barking is contagious and all rational thought suggests that yelling loudly at your dog will be perceived as you joining in. Our poor dogs must think we're maniacs when we get mad at them for not getting quiet when we get loud. But we do it anyway, because that's what agitated primates do: They get loud.

This tendency to get louder seems to be an integral part of our primate heritage, where an ability to make a racket can move you up the social scale faster than buying a BMW. Unlike dogs, one of the ways that chimps get status in the troop is to make more noise than their competitors. But who's the dog with the most authority? It's not the dog who's barking and lunging that impresses me with his confidence, it's the one who gets still and silent. Whatever must dogs think of us trying to get control by doing a canine version of losing it? The difficulty in teaching people to stop shouting and learn other ways of getting their dogs' attention has good dog trainers shaking their heads in one collective sigh of frustration.

But the way we use sound isn't the only challenge we have in communicating with another species. Primate that I am, when I wanted Tulip to come closer, I moved toward her. This is a lovely thing to do to another primate: Moving forward a step or two, perhaps with your hand outstretched, is a friendly, non-threatening way of signaling good intentions. But to a canid? All trainers know that a direct, face-on approach is simply not done in doggy etiquette. Striding forward, head-on, with a paw outstretched? The Miss Manners of dogdom would be appalled. So in primate speak my body said, "Hi! I'd like to make closer social contact with you." In dog speak, it said, "Stop! Don't proceed forward!"

When I switched from "distracted-human-thinking-about-her-dinner-party" to "dog trainer," it was trivial to get Tulip to do what I had asked. I told her to stop doing what she was doing, and then clearly let her know what I did want her to do. Besides previously having trained her (with yummy treats) for stopping what she was doing when I quietly said "no," I also said "come" in dog language, by turning AWAY from her and moving in the direction that I wanted her to go. (Listen to any top agility instructor or good herding dog trainer coach: "Where are your feet?" they all say. They know that your dog wants to go the way that your feet are pointed, while primates that we are, we foolishly point with our paws.) So while I said "come" in a friendly rather than threatening voice, I leaned slightly forward in a canine play bow, turned my body away from Tulip and started moving away from her as I clapped my hands. Irresistible? Well it was that night to Tulip, but if it hadn't worked, I would've stopped calling, gone over to her with something smelly and wonderful (most dog trainers can be identified by the presence of strange odors rising from their pockets) and lured her away by waving it in front of her nose. "Come," and "good girl," I'd have purred as she followed my stinky treat, only giving it to her once she'd left the squirrel and followed me for several yards.

Calling "come" and then running away from a dog as both an incentive and reinforcement can lead to some pretty impressive recalls. My advanced class just succeeded in calling their dogs away from running sheep, sheep poop (oh so edible!) and other dogs getting liver snacks. The dogs had a ball. The humans got a workout. We all smiled like fools.

A good recall is just one example of what distinguishes professional dog trainers from most dog owners. Another is the ability to stop doing what's natural to our species and start doing what dogs can understand. We can train our dogs to understand a multitude of signals that we give them, but why not help them out by learning how our own natural communication system differs from theirs? International business travelers take seminars to learn how their body language, tonality and American customs are interpreted in other countries. Doesn't it make sense to do that with an entirely different species?

So remember that "training your dog" isn't just about your dog. And just as any enlightened dog trainer is generous and forgiving while her dog is learning new things, perhaps it also makes sense to give yourself a break when you find yourself being human. After all, most people who love dogs love lots of animal species, and we're animals too. The next time you catch yourself assuming that your dog can read your mind, repeating a command like an aroused chimp or stopping your dog from coming over to you when you her call to come, just imagine you're watching a nature special on TV about an interesting species—you. After all, dogs seem to like us as much as we like them, and I have the utmost respect for their opinion.

Common Scents

You have more in common with your dog than you think

There's a fox who used to raise her babies every year in a den behind the barn. I say used to, because she's not here this spring. Her absence is probably due to an untimely death from mange. Last year a mange epidemic swept the foxes, coyotes and wolves of Wisconsin, and because our resident fox died in the barn, two of my dogs got it too. I'll spare you the details, but it wasn't pretty. Tulip got it first, having proudly trotted out of the barn with the limp, mangy fox carcass in her mouth. Handsome Cool Hand Luke got it next and worst, and had a hard time looking noble with a naked tail and hindquarters. The five months of quarantine and treatments weren't much fun, and you'd think I would never want to see a fox again.

But I have mixed feelings about the disappearance of my absent fox. Certainly I became conditioned last summer to worry every time I saw a fox. Would it bring mange back yet again? But before the epidemic, which comes and goes like most cycles of nature, I would glory in her presence. Every spring I watched her raise her kits between the road and a steep slope of woods, just 50 yards from my barn. I loved her babies, who played on magical evenings on the front lawn, leap-frogging around the pink and white peony bushes. I loved hearing her cough-bark, watching her trot purposefully across the county highway with food for her young early in the morning.

But even before the mange struck she brought something with her that dampened my pleasure. A smell. A smell so strong and so awful it could gag you. If she'd kept it to herself it'd have been one thing. But she didn't. She painstakingly scent-marked my farm every night, leaving neat little piles of fox poop on my front porch. The piles weren't the problem. My dogs were, because they threw themselves with passion onto her scat and ground it into their ruffs as if it were invaluable. If you haven't smelled a dog who's rolled in fox feces, then your life is slightly better than that of the rest of ours. It's a horrible smell, skunky and repulsive, and it clings to dog fur like a burr.

I can't begin to pretend that I understand what is going on in the brain of my dogs when they're rolling in fox poop. And, of course, it's not just fox feces that gets their attention. Like all dogs, the stinkier the smell, the more attractive the object, including dead fish, fresh sloppy cow pies (the more liquid the better) and partially dried squirrel bodies. Maggots are a plus, a value-added commodity in canine economics. It's impossible not to imagine that dogs enjoy themselves when they're rolling in slime. Their eyes begin to glaze, their mouths droop in a relaxed grin as they duck their shoulders and grind their backs into some foul, rotting mess. After satisfying themselves that they are properly anointed, they trot home with the high-headed, confident stride that we adopt when life is good and the day is ours.

There are myriad theories as to why dogs roll in smelly things, but they're all just guesses. One of the best known is that dogs are putting their own scent on the "resource" to mark it as their own. I don't find this convincing, given that dogs scent-mark resources all the time by urinating and defecating on or around them. (Tulip, who grew up in the pasture as a sheep-guarding dog, still squats in place as she eats her last bit of dinner.) Why not just urinate on the smelly objects like they do on everything else that they want to mark? Others have suggested that, as predators, they are trying to camouflage their scent to prey animals by smelling like something else. I don't know—I wonder then if they'd just smell like a dog or wolf who rolled in something stinky. Besides, if I were a vulnerable prey animal and I smelled an 80-pound dead squirrel moving toward me, I'd probably start getting a little jumpy. But mostly I'm not so fond of this suggestion because of the behavior of prey animals themselves. Working

Border Collies on sheep gives you a good idea of how animals, at least hoofed ones, pay attention to the world around them. Sheep, deer and horses are highly visual, always looking for signs of predators. That's one of the reasons that they have eyes on the sides of their heads—it allows them to "keep an eye out" even when their heads are down to graze. Scent is no doubt important in predator detection in some species, but eyesight is too. I don't think it would make much difference what a crouching wolf or coyote smelled like if he started stalking the flock. So I can't get enrolled in the "camouflage of scent" theory either.

My favorite theory relates to what I call the "guy-with-the-gold-chain hypothesis." It starts with how dogs and other canines make a living. Dogs and wolves aren't just hunters, they're scavengers, and scavengers can't be too picky about getting their meat "refrigerator fresh." They eat what's available, and what's more, they want to live in a territory where there is lots of food available. Perhaps, it's been suggested, dogs roll in dead things or stinky poop as a way of advertising to other dogs: "Hey, look at me, I live in a high-rent district with an abundance of good things." This seems to me to be the most plausible theory.

But perhaps there's something else. Maybe, just maybe, they do it for the same reason we put on perfume. They like the smell. Just as we might apply perfume to attract others, we also wear it to please ourselves. Maybe it just makes them smell good, both to themselves and others. Stanley Coren proposes the same theory in his book, *How to Speak Dog*, in which he suggests that rolling in obnoxious smells (obnoxious at least to us) is the equivalent of the "…same misbegotten sense of aesthetics that causes human beings to wear over-loud and colorful Hawaiian shirts." Somehow it will help from now on, when I'm bathing yet another black and white and green dog, to imagine her in a fuchsia-and-orange flowered shirt, complete with baggy shorts and bad socks.

And what about us? We humans put alien smells on our bodies too. We just like different ones. What must dogs think of a species that grinds up jelly from deer bellies (musk), a squishy liquid from sperm whales (ambergris), secretions from anal glands (civet) and the genitalia of plants (flowers are reproductive parts, pure and simple) to smear all over our bodies. We seem to love this stuff as much as dogs love a good squirrel carcass. Perfume is a $5 billion-a-year industry. New scents are developed in secret research that is as carefully guarded as the development of biological warfare. Perfume and sweet-smelling products like bath oil are, appropriately enough, the ultimate generic gift of Christmas and birthdays. Almost everyone likes to smell good, and to smell good things. That's the aspect of the world of smell that we are very aware of. We notice if the air smells sweet and fresh, or heavy and foul. Bad breath can poison a conversation, and be a social nightmare for its producer. Some of us can yearn for the scent of our lover or child as if hungry for life-sustaining food. Almost everything we buy is scented, whether we notice it or not. Manufacturers do. They know, for example, that furniture polish that smells good is rated as more effective than the exact same polish without an added scent.

Our obsession with good smells isn't new. The athletes of ancient Crete rubbed themselves with scented oils before the early versions of the Olympic Games. Alexander the Great adored perfume and incense, as did all the men of ancient times. Syrians, Babylonians, Romans and Egyptians all favored the scent of flowers and sandalwood and saffron. Indeed, the first gift to the Christ child was incense. So although we ignore the sense of smell in much of our life, we share with dogs a lust for anointing ourselves with scents that make us and others feel good.

What we don't share is what is a "good" smell and what is a "bad" one. It's not just us who are appalled by the olfactory interests of the animal at the other end of the leash. Ever put on perfume or after-shave, your very favorites, and let your dog sniff it? I just put Chanel No. 5 on my wrist, a true classic of jasmine and other floral sweet-nesses, and asked my dogs to sniff it. Luke and Lassie sniffed, turned their heads (and stomachs?) and backed up. Tulip and Pip insisted on ignoring my wrist and sniffing to see if there was food in my fist. Finally satisfied that there was no treat there, they sniffed my wrist and wrinkled their noses. If they could have, I suspect they'd have had me outside under the hose, scrubbing off that disgusting smear of perfume while muttering some doggy version of "Don't blame me for this bath, I didn't grind this disgusting stuff all over your body."

It makes sense that we'd be attracted to different types of smells. It's fitting that omnivores like early humanoid primates, always seeking out plump, juicy fruits, would be attracted to fruity and flowery smells. Dogs are hunters and scavengers, attracted to, rather than repelled by, the scent of ripe carcasses. And in the big scheme of things, one attraction makes no more sense than the other. When you think about it, soaking in plant genitalia or whale goo really isn't inherently any more sensible than rolling in cow pies. Understanding that perspective is helpful when I'm not quick enough to stop one of my dogs from a wallow in some wretched, stinking mess. But frankly, given the power of smell to attract, or in this case to repel, it doesn't help enough. The next time Tulip comes home stinking to high heaven of fox feces, I think I'm going to soak her in a bucket of Chanel No. 5. That'll teach her.

The Right Touch

Where, how and when you pet your dog makes a difference

"Oh, Pumpkin just *loves* petting, don't you, Pumpkin?" Martha said, patting her Cocker Spaniel on top of his head as he tried to investigate the office. Pumpkin's guardian had come to me for some advice about behavioral issues, and was clearly a woman who loved her dog as we all, human or dog, would like to be loved. Only one problem. Though Martha beamed with affection, Pumpkin didn't seem quite so happy. In truth, he looked downright miserable. He kept turning his head away from Martha's hand, trying to avoid her touch, no matter how loving it might have been.

This is not an uncommon scenario: a responsible, caring guardian pets a dog who purportedly adores it as the dog is moving heaven and earth trying to get away. Ask any dog trainer or behaviorist—we see it every day in the office, in classes and on neighborhood streets—people cheerfully petting their dogs, while the dogs look miserable.

Bear with me here. I'm not saying dogs don't love to be petted. Most of them do. But then…they don't. Honest. Dogs love petting and they don't love petting, and both of those statements are equally true. Ironically, the explanation for that seeming contradiction lies in the behavior of those who are actually doing the petting.

Put yourself in your dog's paws for a minute, and it will all make sense. Like most humans, you probably love a good back rub. Just thinking about one can make most of us smile. But you don't want one every minute of every day, do you? What if you're in an important meeting, about to argue against yet another ridiculous downsizing order from your boss? How about when you're playing softball in the league's quarter-finals? Want your honey rubbing your neck when you're up to bat? I don't think so. What if you do want a back rub, but your would-be masseuse pounds on the top of your head like a woodpecker? Feel good? Nope.

Dogs are just like us—their enjoyment of touch depends on when it's offered, how it's done and where on the body it's directed. I'll talk about context first, because it's the variable that guardians most often ignore.

Do you want a massage right now? I don't, I'm busy writing this essay. And I don't want one when I'm training my dog, giving a speech or trying to figure out why my computer does one of the inexplicable and irritating things it does when I'm in a hurry. But I'd love one later, when I've turned off the computer and the chores are done and I'm settled in for the night. Dogs are no different: They most enjoy petting during quiet times, when the pack is settled in, cozied up in the living room or bedroom, the outside world shut away for awhile. They enjoy petting least when they're in high-arousal play mode. Watch a dog who is called away from an exuberant play session and is "rewarded" with a pat on the head—most will turn their heads and move away. I swear I can practically hear them saying "Awww...Mommmmmmmm." Neither do most dogs enjoy being petted while greeting other dogs, eating their dinner or otherwise engaged in something that requires concentration.

And, just like people, dogs vary tremendously when it comes to who they want to touch them. Some are veritable streetwalkers, happy to get cuddly with anything with hands, while others are uncomfortable having strangers touch them at all, at least on the first date. We generally expect dogs to tolerate being touched by anyone, but that doesn't mean they like it. They're just usually not in a position to do much about it.

Dogs are also like people in *where* they like to be touched. Their favorite places may be different than ours—I've yet to see a human go glaze-eyed and thump his leg when scratched above the tail bone—but we don't enjoy it equally on every part of our body.

As I write this, the thought crosses my mind: *Everyone knows this, why use up valuable space talking about it?* And then I think of the thousands of times I've seen people slap their dog on top of the head, or hug the dog until his eyes begin to bulge, and I'm convinced that it still needs to be said. In general, dogs enjoy touch most on the sides of the head, under the ears and chin, on the chest, and at the base of the tail. Although some dogs will turn inside out for any touch at all, most don't like their paws handled, aren't fond of anyone messing around with their hind legs or genitals, and downright hate slappy pats on the top of their head. Of course, every dog—like every person—is different. Some people are particular about where they want to be touched, others are happy to make contact with another warm body any way they can.

How you pet your dog also makes a big difference, and individual preferences are again just as important in dogs as they are in people. In general, most of us enjoy gentle, but firm, strokes and rubs. I wish we'd use the words "rubbing," "stroking" or "massaging" instead of "petting," which is close enough to "patting" to cause no end of trouble. Patting, especially rapidly and repeatedly on top of a dog's head, tends to put him off. (Remember this when your Border Collie drops the ball in your lap for the 560th time. You might as well use this to your advantage!)

This should not come as a big shock to individuals of our species— how much would you like it if a stranger walked up and patted you on the top of your head? In spite of that, people do it to dogs all the time. When I was taping the Animal Planet show *Petline*, a veterinarian-turned-sales rep asked to borrow Cool Hand Luke for a demonstration on dental care. Luke and I had just finished a segment in which I discussed how much dogs dislike being patted on top of the head, and had directed the audience's attention to Luke's look of disgust when we did it to him. Sure enough, after jerking Luke's mouth open several times (as though she was cleaning clams), the women said, "Thank you, Luke," and gave him three short, bouncy pats on the top of his head. We had to stop taping because the camera crew was laughing so hard they couldn't continue filming.

When and how you pet your dog may seem like a trivial issue—I don't expect to see it on CNN *Headline News* any time soon. But it's actually an important one, given the amount of suffering that people and dogs experience when the relationship between them goes sour. Patting their dog's head as a reward for a good recall, dog-lovers everywhere think they are using positive reinforcement, but what they are really teaching the dog—with stunning effectiveness—is *not* to come when called. Before you know it, the dog is at the local shelter because "he just won't listen to me."

Touch is vitally important to the physical and psychological health of both our species, and can even be used therapeutically, as TTouch practitioners and other skilled therapists are aware. We've learned the hard way that babies simply curl up and die if they are not touched, particularly during their first year of life, and I see little reason to believe that an animal as social as a dog would be any different.

Of course, comparing an animal with a human can be dangerous— heaven knows we've all heard the dire warning that the road to hell is paved with anthropomorphism (the attribution of human characteristics to animals or objects). However, the truth of the matter is that it can also serve us well. A few of us in science (including primatologist Frans de Waal and the late cognitive specialist Donald Griffin, for example) argue that we make as many mistakes about animals by not being anthropomorphic as we do in employing it as a strategy. The key is to be objective and analytical, and to use all the information we have about the species in question, along with our own perspectives, to try to understand the experience of another animal.

After all, we rarely know what's going on in the heads of our own family, and they, at least, are members of the same species. But I'll bet you don't greet your spouse or partners with happy slaps upside the head, now do you? So go ahead, put yourself in your dog's place. Who knows, maybe turn about will be fair play—someday, dogs will find that special sweet spot that makes us grin like idiots and thump our hind legs.

You Fill Up My Senses

You and your dog may share a lot, but you live in different worlds

Years ago, I had a dog named Drift who would spend the evening slowly walking across the lawn, head down and tilted, ears pricked. Every once in a while, he'd stop and stand stock-still, head pointed toward the ground. His eyes weren't focused on anything in particular, but his ears were so erect they almost vibrated. Often, after a few minutes of intense concentration, he'd burst forward at a dead run, wind sprint a dozen yards across the grass, and then stop and repeat his slow, low-headed pacing.

Over the years, Drift's behavior entertained a multitude of visitors. Guests and I would sit on the porch, chairs back, iced tea in hand, and speculate on what the heck he was doing. Occasionally, in a fit of curiosity, I'd join Drift on the grass, cock my head and wait for something to happen. Somewhat to my surprise, it did. I discovered how different each patch of grass smelled, and was mesmerized by an up-close-and-personal look at the insects living within the jungle of grass blades. But I don't think I was really able to share the experience with Drift, because he looked like he was listening for something. I listened too, but never heard a darned thing.

But Drift did—I'd bet money on it. There's just no other explanation for his behavior that makes any sense. He couldn't have been sniffing; it's unmistakable when a dog is using his nose, and Drift's nose clearly wasn't engaged. Neither were his eyes focused on anything in particular. But his head was tilted in the way of all mammals when they're listening for the faintest of sounds. Certainly, there are a lot of critters to listen for underneath the grass. Based on the number of moles who bulldoze my lawn every fall, there must be a veritable cornucopia of beetles—the mole equivalent of filet mignon—living under the carpet of green. Why Drift took off running if and when he heard something is harder to explain. My best guess is that he had invented some version of a doggy board game—if you hear something in the grass, run forward twelve steps. If you don't, do not pass go, do not collect 200 chew bones.

Of course, this is all conjecture. I couldn't ask Drift what he was doing, and as importantly, I couldn't know whether Drift was hearing anything or not. We may share an unprecedented bond with dogs, but because our sensory abilities are so different, we quite literally live in separate worlds. In a classic example of "glass half-full, half-empty," dogs and humans are more alike than most other animals, but the realities in which we operate are very different. Every animal on Earth comprehends the environment around her in particular ways, and every animal on Earth both perceives and misses things that others don't. It's easy for us to forget that what we call "reality" is just one slice of the world's sensory pie, bounded by the limits of our species' ability to hear, see, smell, touch and taste.

To a certain extent, this is old news. Every dog lover knows that dogs have a sense of smell that puts ours to shame, and that sometimes they hear things we can't. But it never hurts to remember all the ways in which we differ, and how those differences can interfere with our understanding of our dogs. Vision is a good place to start.

Most of us know that dogs don't see the same colors that we do, but that hasn't stopped us from buying blaze-orange bumpers for working Retrievers or bright-red chew toys for house dogs. These are the colors that stand out best to us on green grass or beige carpets, but we couldn't make them more obscure to our dogs if we tried. Dogs, like some humans, are red/green colorblind—they most likely see red, orange and green as shades of dull gray. They see yellow, violet and blue extremely well, so while a blue toy wouldn't stand out from a grassy background to your eyes, it would to your dog. We've known this for years, but somehow it hasn't filtered down to our day-to-day interactions. I've had dozens of clients who worried that their dog couldn't see well because he couldn't find the red Kong on the grass until he was practically tripping over it. Poor dogs—I wonder what they think of our apparent efforts to confuse them?

Keep in mind that dogs aren't the only ones who can't see all the colors in the world. Truth of the matter is, neither can we. Bees see "ultraviolet" so well that flowers use those colors to direct bees to their pollen. A plain yellow flower isn't plain to a foraging bee, because she can see colors we can't. It's telling, I think, that we don't even have unique names for the colors we can't see: we call them "ultra*violet*" and "infra*red*," perhaps because we can't imagine them in any way except as modifications of the colors closest to them on the spectrum. Given how hard it is for us to imagine colors we can't see, even when we intellectually understand *why* we can't see them, think how hard it must be for our dogs to understand the concept. I don't care how smart your dog is, surely it's too much to ask that he understands that you see colors he doesn't.

There are other important differences between your and your dog's eyesight that influence behavior. Perhaps the most important one is that, while dogs don't resolve images into the sharply defined shapes that we do, they are much better than we are at detecting movement. No wonder dogs can read you like a book—the slightest movement, perhaps imperceptible to you, is a neon sign to your dog. This can be a real advantage if you're aware of how you're using your body around your dog. Great dog handlers are often great because they move their bodies like athletes, understanding that a quarter-inch can make all the difference—whether serving for the match point in tennis or cuing a dog about which obstacle to take in an agility trial. Of course, this ability of dogs to perceive the slightest movement can cause no end of trouble, when we inadvertently move in subtle ways that leave our dogs perplexed yet again by our strange and unpredictable behavior.

For all the differences in the way we use our eyes, dogs and people share something of which you'd think we would be aware. Like us, dogs can be farsighted or nearsighted, and there's every reason to believe it can have a profound effect on their behavior. It makes sense that dogs who can't see who is approaching them would be more nervous than dogs who can. It's meaningful that Chris Murphy at the University of Wisconsin School of Veterinary Medicine found that half of the German Shepherd Dogs he studied were nearsighted, and that the GSDs I see for behavior problems are usually uncomfortable around strangers. Don't get me wrong—in my opinion, a stable German Shepherd is purely and simply as good a dog as ever lived, but every one of us knows that some of them are overly reactive to strangers. Could it be, at least partially, because they have so many problems with eyesight? I use Shepherds only as an example here. There are dozens and dozens of breeds in which a dog's behavior might be influenced by problems with vision or hearing. Murphy's research found that Rotties and Miniature Schnauzers had the same ratio of nearsighted dogs—fully half of the dogs tested were nearsighted. Maybe conformation shows should include an eye chart. I can see it now: "Raise your right paw if the bone is pointing downward..."

Hearing is another sense that is vitally important to humans and dogs, and deficits can also cause undiagnosed behavioral problems. I've seen dozens of unilaterally deaf dogs (deaf in only one ear) whose disability was undetected for years. Although the dogs couldn't localize sound, they could hear with their one good ear so it wasn't obvious that they had a problem. But not being able to localize sound is a bigger challenge than you might think. Imagine not being able to determine the source of a sound. It would make the world seem like a much more dangerous place to a person, and surely to a dog as well.

Besides being easily spooked, especially in new places, dogs who are deaf in one ear often appear to have little focus, and are difficult to train until you understand what's going on. Definitive knowledge of a dog's hearing requires a neurological test (called a BAER test) that usually done at veterinary teaching hospitals, but you can do a quick preliminary test yourself in your backyard. Just stand a good 30 yards or so behind your dog, wait until she's looking 180 degrees away from you, and clap your hands twice. As her head turns toward you, stand stock-still so that she can't use movement to localize you.

Dogs who hear in both ears will look directly at you, but unilaterally deaf dogs will often scan back and forth, only focusing on you after you move, even if it's the tiniest bit.

Dogs who hear well out of both ears hear everything that you can, and a lot more that you can't. Our hearing is best for sounds at the same pitch as speech, or about 2,000 cycles per second. Dogs can hear those sounds well too, but they do their best hearing at higher levels, around 8,000 cycles per second, and can hear up to and above 60,000 cycles per second. Our abilities top out around 20,000 cycles (at least they do when we're young and haven't yet attended rock concerts). It's no accident that the pitch a dog hears best is the same as that emitted by a mouse or a field vole squeaking underground.

That's one of the reasons I first wondered if Drift was listening for digging mammals. Certainly, there's no lack of them here at the farm. With his superior auditory ability, it's possible he was hearing sounds too faint for me to pick up. The problem with this explanation is that all my dogs take great joy in digging up burrowing mammals, and if there had been something furry underneath his paws, the lawn would have looked like a minefield in minutes. That's why I'm sticking with the beetle hypothesis. Maybe he could hear them moving through the earth. It's even possible that they were intentionally making sounds that he could hear and I couldn't. Recent studies have suggested there's a whole world of talking going on in the insect world, to which we've been oblivious. Caterpillars have recently been found to make noises to ants that signal friendly intentions. Good grief, who knows *what's* being discussed by ants and beetles under our lawns.

Maybe that's what Drift was listening to. Or maybe he was listening to something that I haven't even imagined yet. He may have been my best friend, but like all of our canine best friends, he lived in a world I could never completely understand. Keep that in mind when your dog's behavior doesn't make sense—sometimes making sense is all about the senses.

Part Four
TRAINING

THE SHAPE OF THINGS TO COME

In dog training, taking things
one step at a time can make a
world of difference

Maddie was a lovely little dog, with creamy white fur and an open, smiley face. She seemed willing and smart and ready to learn, but her guardian had brought her to me because the dog was driving her crazy. Every time the family asked Maddie to sit and stay, she jumped up and licked their faces. No matter what they did, they couldn't seem to get her to stay still, even for an instant. Someone told them it was because she was trying to assert "dominance" over them. Someone else suggested she'd been abused. Maddie had nothing at all to say on the topic, but kept cheerfully bounding up like a jack-in-the-box every time she was asked to sit and stay.

The same week, I had another client whose treatment plan included teaching his dog Bruno a variety of tricks. The first trick had him stumped, because no matter how hard he tried, and how many tasty treats he used, he couldn't get Bruno to roll over. He tried and tried, and finally came into the office convinced that his dog was deficient.

Getting to the Heart of the Matter
Neither of these explanations had anything to do with the issues at hand. Both dogs appeared to be normal and happy, capable of learning as much as anyone wanted to teach them, and their guardians were dog-loving, intelligent people. The problems, though superficially different, were based on the same important truth: Anything

that we think of as a "behavior," like rolling over or asking a dog to sit and stay, is actually a summation of a great many tiny movements. These incremental movements add up into what we call "rolling over" or "giving a sit signal," each of which is the sum of many parts.

Understanding this—that all actions are actually made up of many smaller ones—can elevate you from a moderately good dog trainer to a great one. The seemingly dim dog Bruno ended up learning to roll over in one session because all I asked him to do initially was to lie down and turn his head toward his tail. Of course, I helped him at first by luring his nose in the right direction with a piece of food, but in no time at all, Bruno was happy to offer the behavior on his own. "Look at my tail for chicken? I can do that!" Bruno began throwing himself down on the ground and enthusiastically twisting his head toward his tail, tail thumping furiously. Next, I asked him to move his head a bit farther back, this time turning it toward his other side, enough that his top foreleg began to rise off the ground. Bingo! More chicken. Step three included luring his head around even farther, until his body followed and completed the roll over in one smooth motion. The humans clapped and cheered, Bruno wagged and grinned, and the pile of chicken pieces rapidly decreased.

Bruno's guardian, a relative novice at dog training, had tried to teach Bruno to roll over by luring his head around with tasty snacks, but because he thought of "rolling over" as, well, rolling over, it didn't occur to him to give Bruno the snack until the dog had executed the entire action from beginning to end. Dog trainers see this problem on a daily basis—people who try to teach a dog to sit up or roll over, and end up throwing in the towel because they can't get the dog to do what they want. This is one of those times when it would help if people were more anthropomorphic (rather than less so as we're often advised). We don't wait to praise our children until they play Beethoven's Fifth Symphony perfectly, do we? Yet that's common behavior with our dogs—we often expect them to do it right all the way through the first time. Anything less is categorized as a failure.

We're even less likely to think of our own actions as the summation of many tiny behaviors. Take Maddie, the dog who wouldn't sit and stay. In the office, I suggested the guardians give it a try so I could see what was going on. The mom of the family stood up, turned to face Maddie, and said "sit" and "stay." As she said "stay," she backed up about a half a step. In response, Maddie sat politely, but then leapt up as soon as she heard the stay signal. "See what I mean!" her guardian said, with no small amount of exasperation in her voice. Next, I asked her to call Maddie to come. You guessed it. She turned to face her dog, said "Maddie, come!" and then backed up exactly as she had when she said "stay." Maddie was paying attention to one small component of the "stay" signal—the backward movement, which she had learned meant "come"—and bless her heart, she kept giving it her best shot, in spite of the confusing response of her humans. It's a miracle they don't bite us more often, truly.

Nothing's Simple

These stories illustrate two perspectives about behavior that can illuminate our understanding of it. One is that a "simple" behavior like asking your dog to sit usually consists of several different sounds and movements, any one of which could be relevant to your dog. We may think that saying "sit" is a singular event, but to an observant dog (and believe me, they're all observant!), there's a lot more going on. You may be concentrating on the word, but as you say it, your hands, head and body are all probably moving in consistent ways, although you're probably not aware of it.

My favorite exercise at seminars is to have a trainer ask her dog to sit, and then ask the audience how many different movements made up that "simple" signal. Usually we come up with at least six or eight movements and one spoken word, any of which could act as the relevant cue to the dog. The last time I played that game, we observed that each time the trainer asked for a sit, she nodded her head ever so slightly. Until her dog saw her nod her head, he would not sit. Once she did, he'd sit instantly. The dog was focusing on the nod, and the human was focusing on the word she was saying. I would bet money if you could've asked the dog to describe the signal for "sit," the dog would've said, "Why, the head nod, of course!"

Bruno, the dog who finally mastered the "roll over" command, reminds us that even one continuous motion—like rolling over—is also the sum of its parts. The general principle of dividing an action up into steps is old news for many trainers, but we can profit from revisiting its importance. Even those of us who are long familiar with what's called "shaping," or the process of reinforcing incremental improvements in behavior, can benefit by remembering that it relates to everything that we and our dogs do.

Understanding that any behavior can be divided up into smaller parts is the guiding principle taught to all students of animal behavior. It was the first thing that I learned from my ethology professors at the university, and it's the first thing good, psychologically-based behavior analysts learn. The fields of ethology and psychology may have very different perspectives, but they agree completely on the importance of understanding behavior as a series of incremental actions. Step-by-step, brick by brick, the foundation of any behavior is built upon little things that add up to bigger ones. The better you are at deconstructing it, the better a trainer you'll be.

BEHAVIOR
INTERRUPTUS

Good habits make good dogs—
teach them early

It's evening, company is coming, your kids are playing chase games through the kitchen, and you just discovered that your dog is busy chewing off the corner of the Oriental rug. Scenarios like this are common, but are rarely covered in dog training books or classes. We trainers like to tell people how to teach dogs to do things, but we don't always do a very good job of explaining how to get dogs not to do something. My new dog Will, especially as a puppy, reminded me daily that raising a dog is as much about teaching dogs what not to do as it is the opposite.

Turn Down the Volume
It's worth taking a moment to discuss what not to do ourselves when a dog misbehaves, because many of our typical responses aren't very helpful. It seems to be oh-so-human to respond to misbehavior by speaking to the dog in words that mean something to us but not to her. How many of us have said, "Be quiet!" to a barking dog and never stopped to think that—unless you're an English-speaking human—the words "be quiet" are just meaningless noises?

Yelling pointlessly at our dogs sounds foolish, but it's a common response when an animal is doing something we don't like. When our words have no impact, we make things worse by repeating them louder and louder, as though sheer volume will clarify what we are trying to communicate. That's true no matter what kind of animal we're talking to—recently, I watched two men try to disentangle a "cattle jam" by yelling, "Turn around, TURN AROUND!" to a frightened cow. Granted, you can teach a cow to turn around on cue, but it seemed doubtful that this particular cow had been the beneficiary of any such training. Remember this story when you are tempted to yell at your dog, and work on getting into the habit of only using words that mean something to her.

Look for Teachable Moments

The first question to ask yourself when your dog is misbehaving is, "What do I want my dog to be doing instead?" You can say "no" until you're blue in the face, but that doesn't give your dog much information. After all, there are a thousand things your dog might be doing wrong, and if you say "no" to one, there are still 999 options left. However, the reality is that there are only a few things that you would like your dog to be doing—so it's a good idea to help him learn what those things are, even when he has other ideas.

Let's take barking at the window as an example. Imagine that you've just settled down to eat your dinner when your dog sees a couple with a stroller walking past your house. He leaps up and launches into vigorous barking and scratching at the window. If you sit at the table and yell "no," you aren't telling your dog anything about what he should be doing instead. Even worse, you are probably adding fuel to the fire by making bark-like noises yourself—what is your dog to think but that you've joined in festivities and that he was right to bark in the first place?

However, what if you quietly select a tasty morsel from your plate (hey, sometimes you just have to be creative), go to your dog and hold it an inch from his nose? Now you have his attention. If you follow up by luring him away from the window and asking him to sit or lie down, you've just shown him what you do want him to do. By interrupting the problem behavior and then redirecting him to something appropriate, you've turned a problem situation into a "teachable moment." Make a mental note that barking at the window could be a problem, and that you need to proactively teach him a different response when he sees people walk by. Use your trusty treats or toys to reinforce him every time he turns away from the window after seeing something outside, helping him when necessary by luring him away or clapping your hands to get his attention. Eventually, he'll do it all by himself, since he's learned that it's rewarding to turn away from the window when someone walks by.

What if you walk into the room and spot your dog munching on the remote control? This is another situation in which you want to interrupt the behavior and redirect your dog to something appropriate—like the chew toy you just bought for him. This is also a time to teach your dog a cue that means "Nope, please don't do that."

"No" is Just a Noise

There's something seductive about the word "no." It's common for people to say "NO!" to their dog and expect him to understand what it means, even when they'd never expect the equivalent with "sit" or "down." As mentioned previously, the word is often yelled at full volume, and sometimes, truth be told, it does indeed stop the misbehavior. Yelling can scare many dogs into stopping what they were doing, but do you really want a dog who is scared of you? Besides, yelling is no fun, so it's worth taking the time to teach your dog a cue that means "I'm sorry, but what you're about to do is not allowed here"—without having to belt it out at the top of your lungs.

First, decide as a group what word or sound you and your family are going to use, and do your best to be consistent when you use it. Work on saying it in a quiet but low-pitched voice. The word "no" is out of favor with many trainers, probably because it is so often abused, but it's a fine choice if that's what comes most naturally. Other common cues are "Wrong," "Uh uh" and "Hey!"

Armed with your handy treats, set your dog up to do something inappropriate, like chew on your shoes. Select an item that will be of some interest, but that's only mildly attractive to a dog—no fair putting down a bowl of chicken. Set the article on the ground, and say "no" as your dog heads toward it. (I'll use "no" for convenience in the rest of this section.) Use a low, quiet voice, but try to have the sound come out of your mouth as fast as it can. You want to surprise your dog with sound, not bowl him over with a scary noise, so keep the volume moderate. If your dog stops moving away from the item in response to your voice, immediately praise him and then give him a treat. If he doesn't, move the treat to his nose and lure him away. Praise as his head turns, and give him a treat. Then back up one step and give him a chance to sniff the article again. If he turns back to the forbidden item, repeat "no," doing all you can to say it before he makes contact. Respond as before, praising and treating if he stops himself, helping him do the right thing by luring him away if he doesn't.

Your dog, bless his furry little heart, will give you lots of opportunities to practice this, whether it's chewing on the table leg, squatting to urinate on the rug or chasing the cat up the stairs. The key to making this work is to say the cue as fast as you can, and then be ready—always, always ready!—to make him happy that he listened to you. It helps to match the reinforcement with what it was he was about to do. If he was about to chase the cat, reinforce him by letting him chase you or a ball. If he wanted to chew on your new shoes, give him an appropriate chew toy.

Good Habits Make Good Dogs

Here's one last comment about preventing dogs from getting themselves (and us) into trouble. I touched on it earlier, but it bears repeating because it's so important. Good dogs are dogs who were taught good habits early in life, and who were prevented (as much as possible) from learning bad habits. Of course, habits can be changed, but we all know it's not as easy as starting from scratch. You'll be happiest with your dog if you are proactive about teaching good habits and preventing problematic ones. This advice sounds so simplistic it almost seems unnecessary, but it takes thought and attention on our part to be one step ahead of our dogs.

If your pup runs to the front window and barks every time he sees someone walk by, teach him a different response (or even better, don't wait for the first bark!). If you have a dog nicknamed "the mouth with paws," don't wait for him to grab your Italian shoes out of the closet. Prevent problems by being obsessive about keeping your personal items off the floor and shutting doors. This may sound obvious, but it takes a lot of energy to be proactive rather than reactive, and it's probably the biggest difference between professional trainers and novices. So give your dog plenty of chew toys, redirect him to what's appropriate and, for your own sake, recite daily "this too shall pass, this too shall pass." It will. And all too soon you'll be wondering where the years went, and you'll forget all the work it took to raise your dog to be good citizen—until you get another one.

Peace, Patience and Pack Politics

The rules of group living apply to all

My client looked at me as though I'd suggested her dogs learn to ice skate. Actually, I'd recommended that she resolve some of the chaos in her multi-dog household by putting the dogs in a back room when company first enters the house. "Are you kidding?" she asked. "I couldn't do that. The dogs would tear the door down."

Oh my. How often I've heard something similar from someone with a pack of dogs whose sheer numbers have begun to cause problems. Perhaps the problem is a bit too much excitement when visitors come to the door—and you're beginning to notice an alarming decline in friends who are willing to stop over. Perhaps there's tension between two of your dogs, and you're starting to worry about where it might lead.

The fact of the matter is that living with multiple dogs is different than living with just one. A single dog may cause no end of commotion when the doorbell rings, but nothing compares to the frenzy that a group of dogs can create when they get overly excited. A riot at a soccer game may come close, but at least sports events have umpires and security guards. (Let's all give thanks that dogs don't spend the evening drinking beer before company comes over!)

Those of us who are stupid in love with dogs, and who are lucky enough to have a bunch of them, know how much joy there is in living with more than one dog. Their interactions with one another are better than the best television show. They take a bit of pressure off us humans to be the "be-all-and-end-all" of their lives and although I find this advantage harder to express, there's something comforting about living within a group, especially if you still have your own bathroom.

Needless to say, group living can have its problems. It's harder to get your dog's attention, much less cooperation, when there are other dogs around to provide social companionship. Some dogs simply aren't suited for living in a group, and are higher maintenance in a pack than when alone. Or they develop blood feuds with other dogs that are so serious that the only silver lining is a dog's inability to build nuclear weapons in the backyard.

Not surprisingly, there's a plethora of advice out there for handling problems that arise within a multi-dog household. The traditional advice, which still appears all over the place, emphasizes the importance of deciding which dog is "dominant" in your house, and treating that individual like royalty. Feed her first, let her out the door first—do whatever you need to do to make it clear that she's more important than any of the other dogs. This advice is based on the belief that the most aggression in a wolf pack occurs when the hierarchy has broken down. The idea is that, if you support the "leader," you'll stabilize the pack. As is often the case, a little bit of information can be a dangerous thing, and the "support the alpha" advice is usually not useful—and can be harmful—to those of us who live with three Shelties and a Terrier rather than a pack of wolves.

First, dogs don't behave exactly like wolves, for which my sheep are very grateful. Additionally, and most importantly, there can be plenty of aggression in a "stable" wolf pack if the alpha male or female is a bully. The wolf researchers I know say that the most important influence on levels of aggression in a pack is the personality of the lead male and female. Some pack leaders are calm, benevolent souls who use force only when absolutely necessary, and don't tolerate the excessive use of it in others. Other high-status individuals are nervous bullies who rule the pack with terror and intimidation. (Any of this sound familiar in our own species?) I've consulted on countless cases in which my clients were told to "support the alpha" and ended up exacerbating problems, not fixing them. Some dogs respond to preferential treatment as if it were a license to bully the others; I've seen homes in which lower-ranking dogs took their lives in their paws, so to speak, just to get a drink of water.

This is not to say that status is irrelevant in a group of dogs. Of course it is—otherwise dogs wouldn't greet one another with tail up or tail down, and it wouldn't matter so much exactly who pees where and whose urine gets deposited on top of someone else's. But I doubt that status hierarchies are as important to dogs as they are to wolves, and most importantly, shouldn't it be irrelevant in your living room when someone rings your doorbell? We don't raise our children to believe that they can get anything they want because of social status (well, at least most of us don't, and those of us who do rarely admit it), so why should we raise dogs that way?

My advice to people who live within a pack of dogs is to teach them that you get what you want by being patient and polite, not by throwing your weight around. Want to go out the door into the backyard? Please pause at the door instead of clipping your human behind the knees and ramming into the geriatric Golden Retriever with whom you share the house on the way out. Want some attention from your human? Please be so kind as to sit or lay down while he or she finishes petting another dog. If you forget yourself, as we all do from time to time, and push the other dog away in order to hoard the attention, you'll be gently reminded to back up, lay down and stay for a bit while all other dogs get special pets under the chin. Excited because there's company at the door? Ah yes, aren't we all, but now that we've grown up we've learned to inhibit ourselves so that we're able to wait politely in another room, or perhaps greet the newcomer a bit more like tea-drinking fans at a tennis match and less like a beer-swilling crowd at a ___ (insert your raucous sports events here).

This may seem like a tall order if you're reading this while your five dogs are at the window, barking and leaping at a passing skate boarder. But it's actually well within your grasp if you remember three things. First, it takes growing humans about 20 years to learn to control their emotions (Okay, some people never do—I encourage them to move to the back room of life), so be patient with your dogs and think in terms of months and years when training, not days and weeks.

Second, turn each exercise into a fun game in which your dogs learn that being patient and polite really pays off—they get extra yummy treats and toys and attention for working so hard. It won't hurt to reinforce yourself for being patient and polite either, something that we too have to practice when our dogs are swirling hysterically at our feet. With lots of positive reinforcement for all of you, good habits become effortless, just like brushing your teeth or checking your rear-view mirror.

Third, start by teaching each exercise to only one dog at a time. Ironically, but understandably, the more dogs we have, the less time we spend with each as an individual. As much fun as it is to live within a pack, you need a relationship with each and every one of your dogs, and you can't get that by always working with them as a group. Go out of your way to work with each dog separately, even if it's just for five minutes. If your dog doesn't listen to you when you're one-on-one, why on Earth would she listen when she's in a crowd? Find out what level of distraction each dog can handle and use positive reinforcement to push the boundaries, ever so slowly, one at a time.

Sure this will take a while, but if you didn't like working with your dogs, you wouldn't have so many, right? It's a rare dog that doesn't love to learn, and most of our dogs seem to adore this kind of training. Besides, just like kids, they love getting even tiny amounts of one-on-one attention from you. Who knows what benefits might ensue—after you've achieved the level of peace and harmony you'd like at home, perhaps you could turn your skills to the fans and players at sporting events....?

ALPHA, SCHMALPHA?

Do you really have to "get dominance" over your dog?

Not long ago, while innocently reading dog food labels at a pet store, I heard a woman carefully explain to her friend that dogs are only happy if you are dominant over them. She went on to elaborate that the way to achieve dominance is to throw a dog onto his back and scream in his face—"just like wolves do," she said. I would like to see her try that in a pen of wolves—no, actually I wouldn't, come to think of it. I don't believe in capital punishment for giving bad advice. And oh, how advice abounds in the world of dog training. Surely it's second only to the tidal wave of unsolicited advice that swells over the parents of newborns. Most people seem to believe that growing up with a dog next door qualifies them to advise the rest of us about any number of dog-related issues, whether trivial or serious, regarding a dog they've never met.

It's bad enough to be surrounded by conflicting advice from well-meaning friends, but it's another when the advice coming from professionals is contradictory. Right now the continuum of advice from dog trainers is as wide as the Atlantic Ocean. One trainer says: "You've got to get tougher on your dog! Dogs only respect the alpha and that needs to be you!" Another says: "Alpha schmalpha, there's no such thing as a dominance hierarchy in pet dogs. Dogs aren't wolves; they evolved from scavenging village dogs who don't live in packs like wolves, so they don't have any understanding of social hierarchies." No wonder our heads are spinning. Not so our dogs. They are quietly licking their paws and if I may indulge myself for just a moment, I imagine that they are amused at our confusion. If they could explain themselves to us, perhaps they would say: There are only two things that you need to know about how to incorporate an understanding of social hierarchy into dog training—first, it's really simple, and second, it's really complicated.

Feel better? Actually, those two statements aren't as contradictory as they seem. Here's another way to put it: Social hierarchies aren't simplistic linear pecking orders, and it's important not to over-simplify them. But the truth is that lots of dog trainers and dog lovers alike have over-simplified the structure of social relationships among dogs, and it's done our dogs no good. Advice about "getting dominance over your dog" has been thrown around like rice at a wedding, without an understanding about what dominance really is.

Most of what we've assumed about the social behavior of our own dogs has been extrapolated from wolf behavior, and these studies have taught us much about the dogs that we live with. Like wolves (who are, we now know, the same species as dogs and can interbreed freely with them), our dogs tend to be territorial and to greet each other in ritualized displays in which visual signals communicate social rank. A submissive grin means the same thing in a dog as it does in a wolf. But extrapolations from wolves to dogs aren't always accurate, given that dogs don't share all of their behavior with wolves. Add on some amazingly inaccurate descriptions of wolf behavior, and you end up with some truly horrific advice about how to treat your dog. For example, owners are advised by some to "do what wolves do and use alpha roll-overs"—grab their dogs by the scruff, throw them over on their backs and scream in their faces. But wolves don't do "alpha roll-overs"—during times of social tension, individual wolves *place themselves* on their backs in a posture called "passive submission." Throwing a dog over on his back and yelling in his face is not "natural" behavior in a dog's or a wolf's social repertoire, it's acting like a lunatic. No wonder so many dogs have bitten their owners when they were subjected to "alpha roll-overs." What would you do if you lived in a house where you never knew when someone was going to attack you? Just like children in abusive homes, as dogs grow up they begin to fight back, and the number of dogs that I've seen who were evaluated as "vicious" for simply defending themselves would break your heart.

So many people have equated the word dominance with harsh training techniques and violence towards dogs that many of us are conditioned to wince when we hear it. The term is so problematic that at one conference, Wayne Hunthausen (a veterinary behaviorist) and I began jokingly referring to it as "the concept formerly referred to as dominance," complete with its own Prince-like icon. Dominance is such a dirty word that even talking about concepts related to it, like social status, risks the equivalent of an electric collar correction from some trainers and behaviorists. But you can't watch two dogs greet each other and ignore the obvious fact that social status is important to dogs—any more than you'd skip up to the President of the United States and ask him for the time. Surely we can avoid using violence on our dogs without pretending that social status is irrelevant to dogs and our relationship with them. After all, all dogs may be equal, but surely some dogs are more equal than others.

A good way to start sorting out any issue that seems muddled and complicated is to step back a bit and look at the big picture. Luckily, although our understanding of the social behavior of dogs is amazingly thin, ethologists know a tremendous amount about how hundreds of species of animals manage their social interactions. That knowledge can help us put our relationships with our dogs in perspective. Here are some things that we know from tens of thousands of hours of observations on animals that live in groups, from coyotes to chimpanzees. First of all, we know that dominance and aggression are completely different things. Dominance is simply a position in the social hierarchy, a description of the relationship between two or more individuals where one individual has more social freedom than the other. This is a familiar concept to humans, being a highly hierarchical species ourselves. You may think of yourself as being egalitarian, yet if the governor dropped by your house while you were reading this essay, you'd probably open the door—but try striding into the Governor's mansion just because you decided you'd like to have a chat.

However, having a social hierarchy doesn't necessitate violence. Of course, violence is one way that an individual can get power, but it's only one way and not a very good one at that. If an individual achieves high social status through aggression, then that status can only be maintained by vigilance and force. Besides, fighting is dangerous, especially for predators like dogs with the equivalent of carpet knives in their mouths, so nature has created another way. Social hierarchies, where each individual has an understanding of his or her place in the society, are designed to avoid violence, not to encourage it. There are many peaceful ways to become a leader in any species from elections (in ours) to family relationships and coalitions (in others).

How an individual achieves and maintains high status is as much a quality of her own personality as anything else. From humans to chimpanzees to wolves to sheep, some individuals can take charge of a group merely by their presence—exuding that hard-to-describe sense of calm confidence that we all are attracted to. I find it fascinating how universal the reaction to "leadership qualities" is and that these qualities seem to be relevant across species boundaries. Every sheep-dog handler is looking for that special dog who, by virtue of nothing more than her physical presence, can convince the sheep to let her take over. It's the less confident dogs who have to use their mouths and nip at the sheep, and it's the truly panicked ones who bite and hang on, eyes screwed shut, jaws clamped on a mouthful of wool. "Alpha-wannabes" I call them, whether dog or human, the personality type that you least want to be your boss, because their insecurity tends to cause them to use force and violence, even when it's unnecessary. Pity the poor dog whose owners are alpha-wannabes. Their dogs can't quit and find another job.

But there's another oversimplification that can also cause dogs distress. This one is from the other end of the continuum from the "get dominance over your dog" philosophy, and it comes from owners who can't bear to deny their dogs anything. Want a massage? Want a cookie? Want to never, ever be left out of anything? It's called spoiling, and although lots of us "spoil" our dogs because we feed them 100 percent natural, organic food and buy them color coordinated dog beds, that's not what I'm talking about. I'm talking about owners who suffer at the thought that their dog would be denied anything. I see them in my office on occasion, and their dogs have literally never learned to tolerate even the slightest frustration. Regrettably, life has a tendency to mess up our plans, so every one of these dogs ends up being frustrated. One minute they can't play with the dog outside because the window is in the way, or they can't get the toy out from under the couch, or their owner pulls them away from the door by the collar. When that happens, some of these dogs have a temper tantrum, never having learned to cope with disappointment. It's one thing to see a young puppy throw a tantrum, but it's downright chilling coming from an eighty-pound adult dog with teeth that can slice open leather.

Some of these dogs are nervous, pacing non-stop in my office until their owners quit catering to them and start taking care of them. The truth of the matter is, some dogs, just like some people, find the world a scary place, and look to their owners for leadership. Leadership is a dirty word in some circles, and that's too bad, because I think that's exactly what some dogs need. Sadly, after 9/11, perhaps it is easier now for some of us to relate to that need for a benevolent leader, someone who can be counted on to make good, wise decisions and keep us safe. But it's hard to convey a sense of leadership if you can't create any boundaries, and so dogs whose owners cater to them all the time are often nervous dogs, dogs who would be calmer and happier if they could count on someone else to make some of the decisions. Alpha-wannabe types of dogs, the dogs who want a lot of social control but are insecure, seem to be especially problematic when they're given no benevolent boundaries.

So although the issues of social status, dominance and how we should treat our dogs are complicated in one sense, in another way they're really simple. Social status is relevant to dogs and people when they live in organized groups with a limited amount of high-quality resources. Dominance is not the same as social status, and social status is just one small aspect of our relationship with our dogs. It's been over-emphasized, misrepresented and used to justify all kinds of horrific behavior towards our dogs, and it's gratifying that many dog owners are turning away from it. But the other end of the continuum can cause its own set of problems. Dogs may need us to be playmates and friends, but they also need us to be benevolent leaders. That's what good parents are, that's what good teachers are and that's what good dog owners are. I guess it's really simple after all.

Plays Well with Others

With practice, even kamikaze dogs can learn some manners

"Oh, he's just *so* friendly, isn't he?!" Larry, the dog in question, was careening around the off-leash park, throwing himself onto every dog within a hundred yards. Size and age were irrelevant—Mastiffs and Maltese alike were on the receiving end of frontal assaults, mounting and body slams. Eventually, our über-"friendly" dog launched himself onto a Border Collie/Labrador-cross who took umbrage, and responded with teeth flashing. No doubt the guardians of the other beleaguered dogs said a silent "thank you!" and—if I may be so bold as to speculate about the mental state of another species—so did the dogs.

Larry's guardian was my client, and after I convinced her to leash him up during our appointment at the dog park, she poured out her frustrations to me. "I just don't understand why dogs are so mean to Larry. All he wants to do is play." This was not a foolish woman—she was a perfectly nice, intelligent person who wanted the best for her dog. She'd never had a dog before, and like a lot of first-timers, she didn't know that, just like children on a playground, a dog can play politely, like a social nerd or like a bully.

Well-trained vs. Well-behaved

It's one thing to have a dog who is *well-trained*—who happily sits on cue and keeps his muddy paws off of Aunt Polly. It's another thing to have a dog who is *well-behaved* around other dogs—who is able to "play well with others," even when the "others" have four paws and furry faces and grab their playmates with their mouths instead of their hands.

A dog may be impolite around other dogs for a variety of reasons. Perhaps he didn't get enough exposure to well-socialized dogs during his own sensitive socialization period. Perhaps the dogs with whom he grew up never explained, in a doggy kind of way, that "no, you mustn't leap onto my head when I'm sound asleep." Some dogs are nervous around other dogs, and express it much like anxious people at a party, who, rather than quietly listening from the sidelines, can't stop talking and end up dominating the conversation. Other dogs might be "alpha-wannabes," status-seeking but full of angst—the kind who has to "get you before you get me." Whatever the cause, what's most important is to recognize rude play when you see it, and either protect your dog from it before he's forced to protect himself, or, if it's your own dog, teach him how to play politely.

Manners 101

First things first—polite play begins with a polite greeting. Well-mannered dogs approach one another at a relaxed pace, from the side rather than head-on. A young puppy may charge full-bore at another dog and slam into her like a test car hitting a cement wall, but by the time that puppy is about six months old, he should be able to approach with a certain amount of discretion. Some pups come hard-wired with this ability, while more exuberant types are usually instructed by their elders to mind their manners. A quiet growl here, a gentle nip there, and most young dogs learn early on that there are boundaries to social relationships.

However, some dogs are oblivious to the warnings of others, don't spend enough time with older dogs, or grow up in a household where a long-suffering older dog lets him do anything he wants. Just as we can spoil young children by indulging their every wish, amicable older dogs can spoil young puppies by allowing them to think that anything goes. I wouldn't worry too much if older dogs gave a nine-week-old youngster "puppy privileges," but I would be concerned if a six-month old dog was allowed to leap onto another dog's head with abandon (and with no comment from the victim) outside of an established play session.

If this is happening in your household, you'd be wise to help your pup learn how to greet other dogs politely. Granted, it's not the easiest project in dog training, since we're talking about behavior between two dogs, not an interaction between you and your dog. However, it can be done, honest.

I've had the most success with teaching dogs a reliable "watch" signal, in which the dog learns to stop what he's doing and turn to look at your face. Other cues—"sit," perhaps, or "lie down"—can work just as well—anything that slows the dog down and distracts him from his uninhibited charge. Practice this first with him alone, and then enlist an even-tempered furry volunteer or two to extend the training. While the other dog is a good distance away, ask for a "watch" (or your cue of choice). When he responds, give him a tasty treat and then release him to go play with his friend. Eventually, you can ask him to watch (or sit) every five steps or so, so that he's alternating his attention between you and the other dog. The essential thing is that you ask him to do something that checks his uninhibited dash toward the other dog. With practice and age, most dogs can develop a relatively refined meet-and-greet style.

Plan A (and B)

Ah, but what if your dog is the victim rather than the perpetrator? You're not helpless here. Even though your dog isn't the problem, the solution lies in teaching her a new trick, an "emergency sit/stay." When a dog comes barreling toward the two of you, ask your dog to sit/stay, and then put yourself between her and the oncoming dog. As the dog races toward you (and your ever-so-polite dog maintains her sit/stay behind you), concentrate on changing that dog's behavior.

People often don't believe me when I suggest that they try this, but an impressive number of dogs have been slowed, if not stopped, by a person flinging her arm up in the universal sit signal, striding two steps forward and saying "SIT" in a confident voice. If that doesn't work, go to Plan B (which I learned from Trish King at the Marin

Humane Society—thank you thank you, Trish!): Fling a handful of treats into the dog's face. While the other dog is snarfing through the grass gobbling up the treats, release your dog and move on, leaving someone else to deal with the kamikaze canine once he's found all the snacks.

Like all training, this only works if you practice it exactly the way you want to use it. That means that your dog needs to learn to sit instantly wherever she is when you issue the cue, rather than coming around to face you (as most dogs are taught), to stay in place as you walk a few paces away, and to hold that sit/stay while you have a conversation with another dog. Clients often are laughing out loud as I describe this, because it seems impossible to achieve. Who could blame them? However, when they work on it step-by-step, using lots of positive reinforcement and gradually increasing the level of distraction, they are often shocked at how much they *can* expect from their dog. Of course, if you try to implement this and another dog goes around you and races toward your dog, be sure to release her—the last thing you want is for her to be stuck on a sit/stay when the playground doofus is about to slam into her.

Recognizing Rude Play

All the above can help with impolite greetings, but what about dogs who greet one another appropriately enough, but then become rude during a play session? Rude play is characterized by lots of body slamming that the other dogs don't seem to enjoy, obsessive mounting attempts initiated by only one of the players, or chase games that seem to be started in order to give one dog an excuse to bite the legs of another.

Because play sessions can be so exuberant, and can include mutually enjoyable growling and sham biting, it can be difficult at first to distinguish rude play from more benevolent interactions. Your best teachers are dogs themselves. Does your dog always end up on top in a play session? Do the vocalizations you hear escalate into low-pitched, serious growls from either dog? Do other dogs try to avoid her? Does your dog love to play with lots of different types of dogs, but starts looking panicky when one particular dog rolls her over? Do the participants appear to be spiraling toward emotional overload?

You'll find that your ability to answer these questions will improve dramatically with practice and with the information gained from books and videos. If you're unsure about what's going on, find a trusted and knowledgeable trainer or behaviorist to objectively watch your dog play with others. Another good idea is to go to a class specifically designed to teach people how to train their dogs to come when called away from a vigorous play session. This is a handy skill for all of us to have in our pockets, and if you take your dog out to the dog park, I'd say it's invaluable.

The basics are simple. Teach your dog the "name game" by reinforcing her every time she looks at you when you say her name. Start with no distractions and then gradually increase the distraction level while asking her to pay attention. Playing with other dogs is the ultimate distraction, so be thoughtful about setting up situations in which you can work on this—you don't want your dog to be reinforced for ignoring you. It helps greatly if you can work on this as a group where each person takes a turn calling his or her dog, and if one chooses not to respond, everyone goes to their dog and the play session stops.

There are several dog training businesses around the country that provide this type of instruction. If your local training group doesn't, you might suggest that they think about it—I've found it to be an invaluable way to help people have a good time at the dog park, rather than, uh…not.

Whether we're talking two legs or four, running into individuals who lack some degree of social skills is inevitable. It doesn't do our dogs any good for us to stand around with our friends and complain about it, nor can we help socially inept dogs if we don't recognize polite (and impolite) play when we see it. Our job is to do what we can to create a joyful but genteel experience when our dogs get together to play. Miss Manners would be so proud.

A Peaceful Walk in the Park

Strategies for defusing tense encounters while walking a dog-reactive dog

"It's okay!" she waves, her two Golden Retrievers racing toward your dog like cheerful, caramel-colored tsunamis. "My dogs LOVE other dogs," she gushes, while your mouth goes dry and your heart stops, then resumes pounding so hard you think it might thump out of your chest. It doesn't matter if the approaching dogs love other dogs—not if your dog barks and lunges every time she sees something with four feet. It's *your* dog who is the problem, and there you are, trying to be responsible, keeping your dog leashed and under control, while those around you let their dogs run free and turn your relaxing walk into a stress test.

Has this ever happened to you? If so, you're not alone. Tens of thousands of dogs (Hundreds of thousands? A million or so? Who knows?) are reactive when they're walking on a leash, and the owners of every one of them dreads the moment when some amiable couple calls out, "Don't worry! Tiger just loves little dogs!" as an Akita homes in on their Jack Russell Terrier like a heat-seeking missile.

I suppose I should be cheered by the fact that so many people optimistically assume that all dogs love others as much as theirs do. It's nice to know the world is still full of people who assume the best, but after hearing hundreds of horror stories from responsible dog owners, it's clear that a little thoughtful caution goes a long way. The fact is, lots of leashed dogs don't do well when they're approached by another dog, or in some cases, when they even *see* another dog. These dogs bark and lunge, sometimes in hysterical excitement, other times in what looks like a murderous rage. In either case, they can make life awfully difficult for their humans, who are just trying to do right by their dog by walking them around the neighborhood. As long as you're not the one haplessly attached to the leash, it's actually a fascinating problem, a perfect example of how a behavior can be caused by a vast range of motivations or emotional states and yet end up looking much the same in its expression.

We all know that lots of dogs are overly reactive on-leash, even when they're the life of the party off-leash at the dog park, but why that might be so is an interesting question. My guess is that either fear or frustration is the driving force for most dogs—fear in defensive dogs of being trapped with no room to maneuver, or perhaps of getting that awful leash/collar correction that so often happens when they start to run toward another dog. Frustration is another common motivator—leashes often keep dogs from doing what they want to do, and it's easy to imagine how that could be frustrating. Certainly most of us have no trouble understanding how frustration can evolve into aggression. (Is there anyone alive who hasn't been tempted to throw his or her computer out the window?) I remember a news story years ago about a man who pulled out a pistol and shot an uncooperative soda machine. Every one I know laughs at this story, probably because we're all well acquainted with the way frustration can spiral quickly into unreasoning rage.

Along with fear and frustration, I suspect that some dogs are simply so excited at the thought of meeting another dog that they go into emotional overload. The joke "I went to a fight and a hockey game broke out" comes to mind. In a few cases I have seen dogs who bark and lunge toward other dogs with the apparent desire to kill them sooner rather than later, but that seems to be a rare occurrence.

Superficially, all of these interior motivations can express themselves in a similar exterior performance. Good trainers and behaviorists use subtle visual signals to get a read on a dog's internal motivation, an evaluation that can be critical when you reach the point of letting your dog interact at close range with other dogs. But any reactive dog, no matter what his motivation, can be taught to walk politely by another dog by learning to respond to two simple signals.

Of course, if you're the person walking the reactive dog, you need to learn them too. After all, there are two of you out there, and given that you're stuck at the other end of the leash, you'll need to work on your own responses. Most of my clients with dog-reactive dogs greet the sight of another dog with an internal "Oh NO!" accompanied by enough adrenalin to fuel a power station. Guiltily, they tell me that they know their dog is picking up on their tension, and that they shouldn't get nervous when they see another dog. Let me go on record right now: If you've learned that other dogs can spell trouble, sometimes big, bad trouble, you've every reason in the world to get tense when you spot Corrigan the Corgi running toward you. Of course, it's true that tension at the sight of another dog moves quickly from one end of the leash to the other, but how else could a person possibly feel? That's the beauty of the two signals I'm about to describe: they will help you as much as they will help your dog.

The first is gloriously simple, so simple that I felt guilty at first when I taught it to clients, worried they weren't getting their money's worth when I gave them the behavioral equivalent of "take two aspirins and call me in the morning." You simply teach your dog to automatically look at your face the instant she sees another dog, and voilà! You've solved your problem. By replacing a problem behavior—barking and lunging—with a positive one in which your dog looks at you in anticipation of a treat—your dog (and you) can switch from "Oh no!" to "Oh boy!" when you see another dog.

"Right," you may be saying, and if your voice is dripping with sarcasm I won't hold it against you. If it were easy, you'd have done it a long time ago. It's not easy—it's just simple, and those are very different things. The process itself takes time and effort, but it's amazingly effective once you know how to get started. Details are important here, so be sure you pay attention to what's happening when you're out on a walk. Most importantly, be proactive rather than reactive, though that is contrary to the way most of us do things. Start working on this issue when you're not out walking your dog.

The key is to start, as all good training should, in an area with no distractions. Just you, your dog and the treats or toys your dog lives for. Teach her to look at your face when you say "Watch" or "Here" (avoid using her name), at first with no distractions, building up after a few weeks to some mildly interesting distractions like someone walking across the street, or a noise that draws her attention. Once she responds 90 percent of the time, start asking her to "Watch" when she sees another dog in the distance, or a familiar dog with whom she's friendly.

Here's one of those important details: Be very aware of the distance between the dogs, and only ask for a "Watch" *before* you think your dog might react. If you find yourself a bit too close to avoid reinforcing that old, bad habit of barking and lunging, turn and walk in the other direction. A common mistake early in training, is to let your dog get too close to another, before yours is ready to perform under such an arousing situation. You want to help your dog learn a new habit, not force her into situations in which she's doomed to fail.

While you're working on "Watch," most dogs will turn to look at your face, collect their treat and go right back to looking at the other dog. That's great, because now they've rewound the tape, which allows you to practice "Watch" again. And again, and again—keep it up for several repetitions, then turn and walk away before your dog begins to get reactive. As she becomes more reliable, you can begin to work on the cue when the distance between the two dogs is shorter. The goal is to ask for a "Watch" every single time your dog looks at another dog, because if you do, eventually she's going to anticipate your cue and turn and look at your face voluntarily.

This is when you pull out all the stops and jackpot her with fifteen treats in a row (sequentially, not all at once) and enough hoopla to impress upon her that she just accomplished the canine equivalent of winning the World Cup. This is what you've been working toward—the point at which the approaching dog becomes the cue. This "autowatch" means that your dog is responding to the sight of another dog by looking at you rather than barking or lunging. Let your dog know, every time she does it, that this response gets an extra special reinforcement from you, and she'll start doing it more and more on her own.

Of course, as we all know, the learning curve is never smooth, and you're going to have setbacks. What happens when you and your dog are blindsided by a dog appearing around a corner a few feet away? Whether your dog starts to bark and lunge or not, if you know the dog is too close for comfort, just turn and swiftly walk in the opposite direction. Don't stop and discuss it with your dog, do not ask your dog to do something that might be over her head, do not pass GO and do not collect $200. Just go. It helps to practice this maneuver too, because when you need it, your brain isn't going to be at its best. Think of how well your brain worked when you were trying to solve complicated math problems under time pressure in an exam. Because adrenalin is not always our friend, practice "emergency" turns so that when you need them, they just happen.

And, oh yes, what about that couple down the block waving and grinning as their dog charges toward yours? It's a bit much to ask your dog to "Watch" your face as some lug sniffs and slobbers all over her, so here's a second strategy. If you have time, my personal favorite is to call out "My dog has mange," or "I think it's okay, she's almost over parvo!" Sometimes you can motivate others to call their dog back, if they can, that is. Many people aren't able to do that, no matter how cheerful their demeanor, so you're likely to find yourself pretty much on your own.

In that case, the "emergency sit/stay," mentioned in the last essay is a good tactic. Teach your dog to stop and stay behind you while you intercept the approaching pooch with a sweeping "Sit" signal or better yet, a handful of treats thrown hard and fast at his face. This doesn't work with all dogs, but you might be surprised at how often it's effective. If you're unlucky enough to have a dangerous dog lurking somewhere in your neighborhood, you might even want to consider carrying citronella or pepper spray. I say this with caution however, because any time you go on offense you run the risk of eliciting defensive aggression. Additionally, sprays can blow back into your or your dog's face depending on the wind, so they're not to be taken lightly.

What's most important is to have a plan of action so that you are as prepared as possible for any contingency. Leaving the house on a wing and a prayer with a dog-reactive dog is like gambling—sometimes it works out, sometimes it doesn't. If, on the other hand, you have some practical tools tucked under your metaphorical belt (collar?), you'll be ready for any contingency. Then you—take a deep breath here—can be the one smiling and waving on neighborhood walks. Whew.

WORDS AT WORK

Learning terms like "positive punishment" can be positively punishing

---

Here's a familiar scenario: You're talking to a woman about a problem she's having with her dog, and she says something like, "All my friends are telling me I should use negative reinforcement and knee Chief in the stomach for jumping up, but that just seems so mean." If you're a professional trainer, you're left trying to figure out how a knee in the stomach could be described as "negative reinforcement," and then you realize that—of course!—she meant "positive punishment." If you're a dog lover who is not steeped in B.F. Skinner's research on learning and current psychology-speak, you might have thought I've lost my mind. How could a knee in the stomach be "positive"?

The truth is that many people misuse the terms associated with operant conditioning. And no wonder. The terms used to describe the four quadrants of operant conditioning—positive and negative reinforcement, positive and negative punishment—are hard to learn. Like riding a bicycle, once you've figured them out, it doesn't seem all that difficult, but getting there requires the intellectual equivalent of skinned knees. When I mention to other trainers how hard it can be to sort out "negative reinforcement" from "positive punishment," I hear what can only be described as relieved laughter.

So there. I'm saying it now. The emperor has no clothes, and the terms used to describe operant conditioning are a pain in the butt to get straight. With apologies to Uncle Skinner, here are some suggestions for sorting them out.

The problem isn't with the terms "reinforcement" or "punishment." It makes sense for *reinforcement* to signify something that increases the frequency of a behavior, and for *punishment* to be something that decreases it. It's not hard to label chunks of organic chicken, liberally handed out at the right time, as reinforcements. And it makes sense that correcting a dog with a choke collar every time he growls at a stranger is a "punishment" that will decrease the number of times he growls at the UPS man, for example. (Of course, it won't make him any less afraid of strangers and might make him more likely to bite, but that's for another essay.)

It's when you add "positive" and "negative" into the mix that the brain begins to wobble. What's logical about labeling a collar correction (or a beating, for that matter) as positive, as in "positive punishment"? In this case, "positive" signifies that something is being *added* to either increase or decrease the frequency of a response and "negative" means that something is being *taken away*. But whose mind works that way? When you hear positive, don't you think "good"? The dictionary says that positive means "confident, optimistic and focusing on good things" or "producing good results." No wonder it's hard to master these terms as used in the psychology of learning.

Ironically, it's psychology itself that explains why it's so hard for us to make the link between "positive punishment" and what it really means. If Pavlov had been involved in creating the terms for operant conditioning, he would have reminded us that we are all classically conditioned to think "good" when we hear "positive" and think "bad" when we hear "negative." Of course, positive punishment isn't always something bad in the sense of hurtful or scary. For example, patting a dog on top of the head when he does a difficult recall is a great example of positive punishment. You're adding something to the system—patting the dog on the head—and because most dogs don't enjoy it, they'll be less likely to come when called the next time. Nonetheless, it's hard to associate the word positive with something one's dog doesn't like.

Perhaps we should create a new lexicon that helps people understand the four types of operant conditioning. I'm not suggesting that we completely replace the standard terms with something else. It's too late for that, and the fact is that if people are serious about understanding and using reinforcement and punishment, they need to be serious about wading through the terminology.[1] However, why not help them out? Anything less seems to be the intellectual equivalent of "Nee-nee-boo-boo, I know something you don't know!"

Here are my suggestions for a new set of terms to help categorize operant conditioning.

For *positive reinforcement*, how about "Add/Increase"? That makes it clear that you're adding something to increase the frequency of a behavior. (Alternate: "Yippy-skippy!")

For *negative reinforcement*, we could say, "Withdraw/Increase" to remind ourselves that in this case, something is being taken away to increase a behavior. (Or, we could go with my personal favorite: "Get out of the rain, you idiot!")

Symmetrically, *positive punishment* could also be called "Add/Decrease," because something is being added to decrease the frequency of a behavior (also known as "You'll be sorry.").

And, last but not least, why don't we think of *negative punishment* as "Withdraw/Decrease," since we're taking away something to decrease a behavior (or, "Too bad! I get to eat the cheese but you don't, 'cuz you didn't sit when I asked you to!").

These are just suggestions—you might be better off making up your own. But either way, don't worry if learning the original terms feels unwieldy. Punishing though it may be, I'm positive that the negatives of learning a new jargon will be ultimately reinforcing.

---

[1] The best resource for learning more about operant conditioning and the real meaning of its terminology is, without question, Pamela Reid's book *Excel-Erated Learning*.

Not Tonight—I Have a Paw Ache

That suddenly cranky pup could be suffering from undiagnosed pain

This is an essay about pain as a cause of behavioral problems. It seems intuitively obvious that pain, and the fear of it, could cause the same problematic responses in dogs as it does in people. The idea that pain is a precursor to bad canine behavior—growling or nipping, for example—is based on sound biological principles. (I'm talking about dogs here, but surely you've done your own share of growling when you felt bad.) Why, then, is pain often the last thing people think of when they hear a Border Collie growl or see a Cocker Spaniel snap?

It's not that folks don't suspect physical problems as an explanation for their dog's behavior. If I had a dollar for every person who speculated that his aggressive dog had a brain tumor, I'd be a wealthy woman. And it's not that educated owners don't consider that a physiological dysfunction—a faulty thyroid, for example—could be the cause and have their dogs checked out by veterinarians. But pain? Simple, old fashioned, ouch-my-neck-hurts pain? Not so much.

Let me give you an example from my case files. A few years ago a client (I'll call her Mary) brought in her dog to be evaluated. Cody was a brown, lumpy mix of a thing, and he'd become increasingly unreliable around people over the previous few months. First, he had growled at a visitor, but over time, he had escalated to biting. In fact, he had bitten Mary that very morning as she reached toward him to clip on his leash. She held out her arm so that I could witness the damage he'd done. I could see dull red streaks on her forearm where his teeth had scraped the skin, and purple and blue bruises swelled under the scratches.

"It's not that he hurt my arm so much, it's that he's always been so good. I could do anything to him, and so could my nephews and the vet. I don't think I ever heard him growl until this started a few months ago. And now I can't trust him anymore." She paused and her face began to crumple. "I don't know what to do." For a while, the only sounds in the office were Mary's quiet crying and Cody's soft panting.

After asking Mary a raft of questions, I began to work with Cody, and it didn't take long for a pattern to emerge. If I kept my hands to myself, Cody was relaxed and happy. If I reached toward his neck, he stiffened and began to growl. This is a common reaction of a neophobic dog who is afraid of strangers, but Cody had been a social butterfly until a few months before, and as far as Mary knew, he hadn't been traumatized by a stranger.

I asked Mary if she'd taken Cody to his veterinarian. "Oh no," she said. "He's fine; you should see him play ball and run around in the woods. He couldn't possibly be in any pain—he just charges around the yard!"

I didn't think of it then, but I could've asked her, "And how do you think I'm doing?" All afternoon, I'd been cheerful and pleasant and full of energy. In the morning, I'd carried slopping-full water buckets and heavy hay bales for the sheep, and had run around in the yard with my dogs. I was a veritable picture of a healthy person. Only one problem—my neck was killing me, and the pain was so tiring that I'd snapped at the dogs earlier in the day (well, not literally). But unless you knew I was uncomfortable, you wouldn't have known why I was short-tempered. Pain is a funny thing. It affects each of us in different ways and at different times. You can be fine one evening and miserable the next. You can be kind and patient with one person, and lose your temper with another.

At the end of our session, I suggested to Mary that she talk to her veterinarian, and good for her—she took Cody to the clinic soon after. She called me a week later. "I can't believe it! Cody's not growling or snapping anymore. My vet found that he had injured his neck and was in a lot of pain. He had a chiropractic adjustment, is on medication and is doing wonderfully!"

This neat, happy story sounds almost too good to be true. It is true, but it's also worth noting that it's rare for things to work out so tidily. I'd love to tell you that all my clients find that their dogs were grumpy only because they had torn ligaments or pulled muscles. Sorry, that's not how it works out. The fact is, most behavioral problems are not medical ones. More often, dogs who growl at strangers because they are afraid of them are not ill, they are fearful. Just as dogs who guard their food bowls and snap at their guardians aren't sick, they're just, well, guarding their food bowls. However, if a dog like Cody, a long-time model citizen, suddenly starts behaving in new and negative ways, it's time to talk to the vet.

This essay is not just for people who own dogs. I'm also addressing these remarks to veterinarians. I say that with the respect due to a profession that has extended and improved the lives of at least a gazillion dogs. However, over the last 20 years, I can't tell you how many dogs I've seen who were cleared by their vets as being "fine," only to learn later that the dogs were in pain. I want to be very clear here: I am not a vet and I can't and don't diagnose medical problems. I'm a Certified Applied Animal Behaviorist who sends some of my clients back to their veterinary clinics or their animal chiropractors for another look to see if their dog just *might* be in pain.

You can't blame the medical profession for struggling with this issue. It's notoriously hard to diagnose pain. It doesn't show up on x-rays or MRIs or CAT scans. You can't get a positive blood test for "pain." It's a completely subjective experience that can come and go, and many of us (much less our dogs) aren't always honest about it. I remember my mother in her last years, complaining vociferously to her daughters about how much pain she was in—except during appointments with her doctor, when she smiled and laughed and reported that she was "doing great!" I suspect that happens on examining tables in vet clinics too—our dogs grinning and wagging until they come home and get grumpy again under the dining room table.

In my experience, pain may not be a common cause of growling or snapping but it deserves consideration. Think about it before you start speculating about brain tumors or attributing complicated motivations to your dog's bad temper.[1] I'd write more, but I've got a headache.

---

[1]Don't *ever, ever* give your dog pain medication without talking to your veterinarian. Some common human pain medications can harm or even kill your dog.

Take Two Giggles
and Call Me in the
Morning
Enrichment activities are
stimulating for you and your dog

If you love your dog, you owe a lot to the lowly rat. That's rat as in rodent, not as in Rat Terrier. In addition to being the front-line soldiers in decades of learning experiments, white laboratory rats taught us how important an enriched environment is to the life of a healthy, normal dog.

Researchers found that the brains of rats raised in sterile environments developed differently than those of rats raised in enriched environments. It seems that the lack of stimulation led to a congruent lack of connections between brain cells (called "dendritic branching"). Researchers quickly learned that this phenomenon not only affected individuals of many species, but that early deprivation led to profound and often irreversible effects on their behavior as adults.

And what does this have to do with the pup at your feet who just got back from flyball class, gets organic free-range chicken every night and has a bevy of interactive toys that rival those found in a kindergarten classroom? Lots, because knowing how much stimulation an animal really needs is important to those of us who want to do right by our dogs but can't afford to retire and spend our entire day in their service.

The beginning is a good place to start, and here the message is crystal clear. Puppies who grow up in sterile, unvarying environments have a higher likelihood of not being able to cope with any kind of change as adults. Ironically, this means that many of the kennels that most impress the public are the worst possible environments for a developing puppy. When I talk to my clients about where they got their puppy, I'm struck by how many of them stress how clean the kennel was. "Did the puppy get out and about on the grass, in the house, on the gravel driveway?" I ask. They often don't know the answer to that question, but they know that the kennel floor looked spotless.

Americans are obsessed with the appearance of cleanliness (just ask a European). We don't allow dogs in restaurants, on buses or in stores, even though most of us have one or more in our kitchen. The motivation for this tradition was not a concern about dog bites, it was the belief that dogs are dirty and might spread "germs." Once we discovered that "germs" are everywhere and that some of them correlate with certain diseases, we went on an all-out war against them. "Cleanliness is next to godliness" pretty well sums it up. Americans became so fixated on cleanliness that an early and profoundly influential behaviorist, John Watson, actually advised mothers never to kiss their babies. Kissing spreads germs and was therefore to be avoided at all costs. (Not to mention that it probably reinforces problematic behavior, a double whammy that could lead, in his words, to "invalidism" in a child.)

Thus Americans learned to get a puppy from a clean environment, because a clean environment meant a better chance of a healthy puppy raised by responsible breeders. And there's no doubt that a clean environment is important to a healthy puppy. But the extreme of "clean" is "sterile," and sterile, it turns out, is only valuable if you're doing surgery. Sterile environments provide so little sensory stimulation that they literally deform developing brains. So the lesson from our poor, long-suffering laboratory rat is to balance cleanliness with environmental variety when choosing or raising a puppy.

When I bred Border Collies, my puppies had been on towels, carpets, straw, grass, gravel and wood floors by the time they were four weeks old. I kept their puppy pen as clean as I could, but I was just as concerned about providing them with variety as I was with keeping them clean. At five weeks of age, they went on clumsy adventures up the rocky hill path, through the grassy sheep pasture and down through the woods. Granted, it took us half an hour to do what was usually a 10-minute walk, but I spent the time being charmed, and the puppies developed essential neuronal connections that would help them cope with both major and minor stresses (read change) as adults.

Sterility is an equal-opportunity employer; it's not just puppy-mill puppies growing up in hanging wire cages who suffer from it. I've met far too many dogs from "reputable breeders" whose dogs live in kennels 24/7 and whose puppies get good healthy food, spanking clean kennels and little else. Don't get me wrong, I have no problem with dogs living in kennels if they get lots of time out to learn, socialize and explore the world. Neither am I advocating getting your puppy from some squalid *Deliverance*-like setting. I am saying that we need to do a better job of educating breeders and buyers about the importance of environmental enrichment during canine development. (Keep in mind that you can take this too far and do harm to a puppy by overstimulating him. Puppies, like infants, need lots and lots of quiet naptime. A little bit of adventure goes a long way with a six-week-old pup.)

But what about mature dogs? If you have an adult dog, or like many of us, an entire pack of them, how much "environmental enrichment" should you be providing? This is, of course, a tricky question, because the answer depends upon the breed, age and personality of your dog. A one-year-old Border Collie needs about 100 times more stimulation than a six-year-old retired racing Greyhound. Or would that be 500 times? Let's just leave it that adolescent individuals of working breeds require just about as much physical exercise as you can provide.

But physical exercise is only one component of the stimulation a dog needs every day. It seems everyone knows that their dog needs to be physically active for part of the day, although too many people define "activity" as a short on-leash walk around the block. (Snore.) Brains need to be exercised too, and that's where many of us could do better by our dogs. Dogs evolved to solve problems and make decisions: Should we go hunting here or over there? Should we start running at the herd now or wait until they get closer? Will my aunt let me snatch of piece of the elk we just killed, or should I wait?

There's nothing like learning something new to stimulate a brain, so if you're wondering about the quality of your dog's life, ask yourself what new information your dog has had to master in the recent past. If you have multiple dogs, try teaching all of them a new trick (and enjoy comparing how each of one them learns differently and at a different pace). The beauty of tricks is that you can teach them in any kind of weather, no small advantage in some parts of the country, and you can always come up with a new one. It doesn't take much of your time, and a little bit goes a long way. I learned the value of training tricks one brutal Wisconsin winter when the chill factor was 50 below for days on end. That's a bit much even for me and the Border Collies, so in a desperate attempt to keep my working dogs busy, I substituted trick training for long walks in the country. To my amazement, they seemed more relaxed and slept longer after 20 minutes of that than they did after a walk twice as long.

When you think about it, it makes intuitive sense. We get tired when our brains are learning new things, and for good reason. When you're learning, you're using your brain's frontal cortex, an energy hog that beats SUVs hands-down for its fuel needs. Once you've learned a behavior, the mental machinery that powers it moves from the frontal cortex into other areas of the brain that consume less energy. Pretty slick system, and a good reminder of why learning something new can either overpower a dog (if too much) or enhance the quality of her life.

But new isn't all that's important. If you love doing something, it doesn't have to be new to be fun. I'm always amazed at agility class participants who think their dog would be bored by the next session of agility because they won't learn anything new. This is usually said by someone whose dog adores agility and can barely wait to get onto the course. The obsession with dog classes presenting new material every week, a common refrain heard by trainers from class participants, doesn't make any sense when you think about it. If you love tennis or golf or walking in the country with your dog, your enjoyment isn't dependent upon whether you learn something new each time. What's relevant is whether or not you love doing it. We could all use a little more fun in our lives, and so could many of our dogs. Dogs like to have fun too, and it's up to every responsible dog owner to provide it for them. Of course, what fun looks like depends on your dog—it might be hunting mice or playing ball or dashing through an agility course—but light-hearted play is good for the soul in all of us. If you need help figuring out what lights up your dog's eyes, just ask yourself what it is your dog does that starts you giggling. There's nothing more engaging than a dog having a rip-roaring good time, and if you start laughing on the outside, there's a good chance your dog is laughing on the inside.

The question remains: How much of all these things do dogs really need? Should we feel guilty if our dogs' day doesn't include two hour-long walks off-leash in the country, an hour of trick training, lots of time playing with all those cool new interactive toys, a cozy nap on an orthopedic bed in the afternoon and flyball class at night? Well, you could, but I wouldn't. Yes, that would be a wonderful day for a lot of dogs and while it would be a wonderful day for their humans too, most of us just can't manage it. Sometimes I think the world of dog lovers is divided into two groups: those who think a good dinner, a yearly vet visit and a walk around the block is a good life for a dog, and those who can't do enough for their dogs, dedicating all their spare time to their pooches' health and entertainment.

Surely the key here is balance—a life that includes a certain amount of routine balanced with some surprise and adventure, a certain amount of rest balanced with the stimulation of mental and physical exercise, and daily doses of pure, exquisite fun. I can't tell you how much of that your dog needs. (Sorry. That's the question I'd be asking right now!) The answer depends too much on your dog as an individual for a generalized prescription to be of any value. But it also depends on your ability to provide for him or her, so unless you're living a life of luxury, I wouldn't indulge in feeling guilty because you can't do everything you'd like for your dog. Just remember that our friends need to keep their brains and bodies engaged on a daily basis, even if for brief periods of time, and just like us, they'll be happiest if you can help them find that exquisite balance of quiet contentment and joyful exuberance. So ask yourself if your dog is getting mental and physical exercise, the stimulation of learning new things and a good solid dose of fun. If she is, good for you. If not, don't become wracked with guilt, just figure out what you can reasonably do to improve things. Meanwhile, go have a giggle with your dog for me. (Insert here, Cyndi Lauper singing "Dogs just wanna have fu—un!")

Part Five

GENETICS, ETHOLOGY AND BEHAVIOR

CANIS COUSINS?

Unraveling ancestral ties

Dogs aren't wolves, pure and simple. Except, uh, they are. Sort of. Sometimes.

Lest you think I've lost my mind, I'd like to explain why the statements "dogs are wolves" and "dogs aren't wolves" are equally correct. I'm writing about this issue because it's inherently a confusing one, and if we really want to understand our dogs, it's important to get it right.

I say it's a confusing issue because even the most casual of readers can find authors who authoritatively argue for one side or the other. Innumerable articles and books have stated that the way to understand dog behavior is to understand the behavior of wolves. For example, in *Leader of the Pack*, authors Baer and Kuno say "… dogs continue to remain instinctively loyal to an autocratic leader, holding a mind set identical to that of their cousin, the wolf." Perhaps most tellingly, Roger Abrantes' book, *Dog Language*, is illustrated primarily with drawings of wolves.

But the opposite viewpoint can be easily be found in recent writings. In the book *Dogs*, authors Laura and Raymond Coppinger argue: "But dogs can't think like wolves, because they do not have wolf brains." What's going on here? Roger Abrantes and Raymond Coppinger not only both have a Ph.D in relevant fields, they both have spent their lives interacting with dogs. Surely they must both know what they're talking about. They do. It just depends on what behavior you're looking at. Of course dogs *are* like wolves in many ways—how could they not be? Wolves are dogs' closest genetic relatives and immediate ancestors, and we know that much of behavior is heritable. But there's a reason wolves aren't allowed in family-dog training classes—treating a wolf exactly as you'd treat a dog is a fool's game at best. What's important if you want to understand dog behavior in any depth is to know when it's true that "dogs are wolves" and when it's not.

Dogs and wolves share a remarkable number of behavioral traits, the most obvious being their visual signals. There's a good reason Roger Abrantes used the visual signals of wolves to illustrate social communication in dogs—their signals are virtually identical. They use the same postures and expressions to signal status, to appease others, to express fear, excitement and playfulness, to name a few.

That's just one way in which dogs are wolf replicates. In a study done by Eric Zimen, one of the world's authorities on the behavior of wolves, dogs and wolves were found to be exactly equivalent in their grooming behavior, courtship behavior, delivery of newborns, nursing behavior and infantile behavior.

This all makes perfect sense, given that dogs and wolves are more than just kissing cousins. Always considered closest relatives, they have recently been reclassified as the same species. Historically, they were given different Latin names (*Canis familiaris* and *Canis lupus*), but they didn't actually fit the biological definition of separate species. Animals are considered to be of a separate species if their progeny can't reproduce. Reproductive inviability is the result of there being too many genetic differences for each parent's chromosomes to line up during the process of genetic combination. That's why horses and donkeys are classified as separate species—a horse bred to a donkey results in a mule, but mules can't reproduce themselves. It's an evolutionary dead end. But wolf–dog hybrids are common, and can continue to reproduce no matter how many generations are combined. Taxonomists finally paid attention, and reclassified wolves and dogs as both belonging to the genus *Canis lupus* (but as different sub-species, *Canis l. lupus* and *Canis l. familiaris*.)

Dogs may be the same species as wolves, but they are still profoundly different from them. People who have spent time around wolves always mention how inquisitive, active and smart wolves are, with the subtext being "compared to dogs." If you're a dog lover like I am, don't be offended. I am stupid in love with dogs, but I've walked away from wolf–dog hybrids amazed at how different they are from dogs. I worked with a five-month-old, 80 percent wolf–dog hybrid who was simply beside himself in his owner's tiny apartment. In the hour I was there, he never stopped climbing (on me, the coffee table, the walls...), never stopped using his mouth (on me, the coffee table, the walls ...) and never stopped looking for something to do (with me, the coffee table, the walls...). This was far beyond the normal activity level of a high-energy and bored puppy. This felt like a whole other animal altogether. It was.

Wolves aren't just active and inquisitive. People who work with them take every opportunity to remind us that wolves are wild animals, period. That means that they are rarely house trained, can't be kept off the furniture and can't be punished for getting into the garbage. Wolves have their own set of social rules, which they take very seriously. Punishment for getting into the garbage would be perceived as an unprovoked attack, and would be responded to in kind.

Ray Coppinger tells a wonderful story in the book *Dogs* in which wolf expert Erich Klinghammer of Wolf Park fame told him to treat the wolves he was about to meet as if they were dogs. Ray heartily thumped an adult female wolf on her side by way of an enthusiastic greeting, which resulted in an equally enthusiastic attack on his forearm and another wolf tearing at his pants. Granted, those of us who work with aggressive dogs have dropped enthusiastic thumps from our greeting repertoire, but there are plenty of dogs who love them, even from strangers. Not wolves.

Possibly the most important area of comparison between wolves and dogs is the role that hierarchies play in their social structures. This is the most controversial aspect of wolf/dog comparisons, and understandably so. It's mentioned most often, but is probably least understood. How often have you read that "you've got to get dominance over your dog!" with references to the social structure of a wolf pack?

Dog lovers have been advised to solve an infinite spectrum of behavioral problems by "getting dominance" over their dogs. But the problems with this approach are legion. First, the concept of dominance, as mentioned in an earlier essay, is poorly understood, even in a wolf pack. Many people equate dominance with force and aggression. Being the dominant individual of the group, or being the one with the most social freedom, is a way to avoid aggression, not an excuse to use it. Social status can be obtained with or without force—Gandhi and Saddam Hussein were both dominant individuals in their culture at one time, but they got there by completely different routes.

Secondly, even in a wolf pack, dominance doesn't get an individual every single thing that he or she wants every single second of the day. It's just not that simple. If you have it, it gives you more social freedom than others, but that doesn't necessarily give you license to do anything you want any time you want it.

Another problem is whether the social system of dogs really is equivalent to that of wolves. It's been argued that we shouldn't expect dogs to show any type of social structure akin to that of wolves because dogs evolved as scavengers instead of pack hunters. Scavengers don't need closely knit packs to make a living, since digging up trash in a garbage dump doesn't take a coordinated group effort. But you can't credibly argue that hierarchies are irrelevant to dogs—the awareness of a social hierarchy is as much a part of dog behavior as is tail-wagging and ball play. But just like wagging tails and fetching balls, individual dogs vary tremendously in how much they engage in them. Some dogs wag their tails all the time, some rarely. Some dogs would kill themselves playing ball, others couldn't care less.

I think that dogs and wolves are similar in that social hierarchies are part and parcel of who they are, but I think they differ in at least two ways. First, social status may be relevant to dogs, but it's less important to them than it is to wolves; and second, individual dogs vary more than wolves in how important status is to them. Here's the logic behind those statements: We know that dogs behave most like juvenile wolves—they're the Peter Pans of the wolf world. Dogs never really quite grow up, which is why they stay more docile and biddable than adult wolves. As individuals who never quite grow up, it seems likely that dogs wouldn't take social hierarchies quite as seriously as their adult wolf cousins.

Less intuitively obvious is that the process responsible for creating eternal adolescence also creates a high degree of individual variability. "Paedomorphic" animals are reproductively mature individuals who still look or act like youngsters, and it turns out that selecting for such a phenomenon also selects for a high degree of variability. That's one of the reasons it's so easy to create Great Danes and Chihuahuas from the same gene pool. But it's not just size and structure that's variable in our domestic dogs, it's also behavior and temperament. The importance of who's who in the hierarchy varies tremendously from dog to dog, as do, for example, interests in herding sheep or retrieving game birds.

And so, I return to my earlier statements, "dogs are wolves" and "dogs aren't wolves," and the fact that they are equally true. Perhaps one way to look at it is that dogs are baby wolves who have adapted to living with us in our world, and wolves are wild animals who can adapt to letting humans live in theirs. Keep this in mind the next time you read a wolf/dog comparison, always asking yourself exactly what is being compared. Don't let their simultaneous similarities and differences throw you. After all, oranges are different than grapefruit, but it's important to know that they're both citrus fruits. And just like different types of citrus fruits, dogs and wolves are very similar, but ultimately very different. So give your furry, little orange a pet from me, and viva la différence!

THAT WAS THEN, THIS IS NOW

Beyond the "dominance" paradigm

It happened in Scotland, where I attended a conference on animal welfare in the 1990s. My host had escorted me into a crowded room at cocktail hour, and then tapped a spoon against her glass to get the group's attention. "Everyone," she said, as the crowd turned and looked toward us expectantly. "Everyone, please meet Dr. Patricia McConnell from the States. She's an ethologist." At the word "ethologist," a collective "ooooh" floated toward me from the crowd. I might even have heard some "ahhhhhs"! It wasn't me who got the reaction, it was my profession. Everyone seemed to know what ethology was, and most importantly, was eager to talk about it. In short order, I was surrounded by individuals enthusiastically discussing animal behavior, everything from the mating rituals of ruffled lemurs to the antics of the Labrador Retriever in their living room.

I think of that evening in Scotland when I am introduced as an ethologist here at home in the US. More often than not, the word is changed into "ecologist," as if somehow we had collectively developed a kind of a lisp, and had really meant ecologist all along. "Ethology" isn't a term that's widely familiar in this country, and I wouldn't mind that so much if this lack of awareness hadn't led to the mis-use of the term as it relates to dog training.

This most often happens when people with no academic background cite ethology as a justification for "getting dominance over your dog" as a way of solving all behavioral problems. To the collective amazement of many of us in the behavior and training field, methods emphasizing this perspective have recently cropped up again in this country. Does your dog not come when called? Does he urinate on the carpet? Well, then, we're told, that's because you haven't established a clear pack hierarchy.

But what would dominance have to do with coming when called or peeing on the rug? Dominance is about who gets the bone if there's only one available and everyone wants it equally. There's no logic in explaining away every behavioral issue as being related to dominance or submission, just as it would be illogical to excuse one's own bad habits using the concept of social status. Good luck with explaining that you ate three pieces of fudge cake because you're confused about your place in society.

Advocates of the "getting dominance over your dog as the answer to everything" perspective often support their argument by citing scientific evidence—especially data from ethologists—that dogs are pack animals. As such, they argue, dogs don't need love from us, they just need to know their place. Sigh. About the only thing that's true about this argument is that dogs are indeed highly social animals. And it's true that we learned that from ethologists.

Ethology is the study of behavior, with an emphasis on an animal's behavior in its natural environment. The current use of the word began in Europe in the 1930s, when Konrad Lorenz, Karl von Frisch and Niko Tinbergen began the work that would eventually win them a Nobel Prize in 1973 for their studies on behavior. These European scientists were especially interested in observing animals in the wild, as opposed to the then-pervasive American practice of studying animals' behavior in captivity. Eventually, this type of fieldwork led to David Mech's vast body of research into wolf behavior, and to Jane Goodall's forays into Africa to observe chimpanzees in the wild.

One of the many aspects of behavior that interested these early ethologists was social organization, and much of their initial work attempted to understand how animals related to one another and how they organized their social relationships. It is true that, in the '40s and '50s especially, ethologists were fascinated by issues related to social hierarchy and status. It was also during those same decades, 50 or 60 years ago, that much was written about dominance (male dominance in particular), as well as about the function and evolution of aggression. That doesn't mean these issues are the only ones ethologists are interested in, it just means that back then, matters related to status and hierarchy got a lot of attention.

At the same time that ethologists were discovering social hierarchies in a multitude of species, American animal behaviorists were dispensing food treats and using electric shocks on mice, rats and monkeys to understand the learning process in animals. Along the way, things were done to animals that most of us would rather not think about. The reason that educated behaviorists and trainers are convinced that positive reinforcements (like tasty snacks) are more effective in dog training than "positive punishment" (like electric shocks) is because thousands and thousands of animals were experimented on in ways that would never be allowed today.

Although I wish I could go back in time and prevent some of the suffering that was caused by these experiments, it is true that much good has come from them. Just as modern-day ethologists build on the early work of Lorenz and Tinbergen, learning theorists and psychologists have profited greatly (as have dog trainers) from the early work of American behaviorists like Watson and Skinner. However, it doesn't mean that today's psychologists advocate using electric shock on your dog any more than ethologists advocate using force to achieve "dominance over your dog."

People who argue that ethology supports "getting dominance over your dog" are not only focused on an issue more relevant 50 years ago than today, they are misrepresenting the findings of early researchers on social hierarchy. Social hierarchies are complicated things that allow animals to live together and resolve conflicts without having to use force every time a conflict comes up. Social status is but one of many factors that influence an animal's behavior, and it only relates to an animal's behavior in specific circumstances. It's relevant, I would argue, when dogs are greeting one another, when they are in potential conflict over who gets the bone or who goes out the door first, but it's irrelevant when a dog is deciding to come (or not) when called. High status wolves don't bark out a COME! command to subordinates, and they don't punish young pups for "disobedience" if they don't do a perfect recall when asked. Status just isn't relevant in most social interactions. Further, studies on a raft of social species have made it abundantly clear that relationships between individuals are based as much on individual personality and learning as they are on social status.

Thus, using "dominance" as a foundation of a training program ignores all that ethologists have discovered about the nuances of communication and social interaction, and all that psychologists have come to understand about the learning process. Ethology is no more about "getting dominance over your dog" than psychology is about using electric shock to influence behavior. Both scientific perspectives provide us with a rich and textured foundation that informs academics and dog-lovers alike. From understanding subtle visual signals that tell us when our dogs are anxious to knowing when to reinforce our dog's behavior and when to withhold a food treat, ethology and psychology can work hand-in-hand to help us improve our relationships with our dogs. Neither advocate using force or physical punishment as the primary method of training dogs.

The next time someone tries to seduce you with bad science by saying that "ethology justifies using force to control your dog," don't hesitate to challenge them. Science is on your side—put Lorenz and Skinner in your pocket and use what we've learned in both ethology and psychology to enhance, not diminish, the relationship between you and your dog.

BEAUTY IS ONLY FUR DEEP

Bad (and good) behavior can be passed on

They sat white-faced in my office, as afraid of my advice as they were of their own dog. They loved him dearly and only half-jokingly called him their "other kid." The thought of putting down such a beautiful animal was simply unbearable. But their fear of him was growing stronger than their love. Kinko's growling and barking at visitors was bad enough, but now he'd become aggressive toward them too. He'd bitten each of them when they'd tried to pull him back from the door when company came. The most-recent incident, when he sank his teeth deep into Carol's forearm and shook it as though he'd caught a rat, was the last straw.

During the evaluation, I asked about Kinko's early history. "Do you know anything about the behavior of his parents?" I asked. They shook their heads from side to side. "No, we don't," Paul said. "Well, we did see them from a distance," his wife Carol explained, "but they were barking and snarling so much we were afraid to get anywhere near them, so we really couldn't say anything about their behavior."

Sigh. I wish this was an isolated case of particularly naive owners, but in one sense, it's not. Kinko's owners weren't the first clients I've seen who didn't relate the behavior of parent dogs to the behavior of their pup. I've worked with multitudes of intelligent, articulate people—from physicians to CEOs to professors—who sat in my office and made it clear that they had no concept of the heritability of behavior. Everyone knows that retrievers retrieve and that herding dogs herd, but beyond that, the genetics of behavior is a great mystery to the average dog owner. My clients knew enough to expect that their Labrador would love to play ball, because that's what Labs are supposed to do. But they didn't know enough to relate the barking and snarling of the pup's parents to the behavior of their offspring once he grew up.

As I write this, I'm second-guessing the topic of this essay. Surely everyone knows that the best predictor of a dog's behavior is not his breed or his soulful brown eyes, but the behavior of his closest relatives. Am I wasting our time, stating the obvious? And yet, I'm not making up all those clients. Good people, smart people, dog-loving people, who tell me, day after day, week after week, that no, they didn't think to ask about the disposition of the pup's sire before they brought his daughter home.

Examples of behaviors that are passed on from parent to pup are endless. My first Border Collie, Drift, expressed excitement by lifting one forepaw at a time, alternating left and right in a staccato tap dance. I've had a lot of dogs since, and they all have their own ways of expressing excitement. Tulip the Pyrenees spun in a circle, eyes shining like firecrackers. Lassie dashes off to pick up a toy and returns it to me, shaking it furiously. But only Drift's son acted just like his father when I said "Let's go to the barn," tap-dancing like Fred Astaire in his black-and-white furry tuxedo.

Who would expect that the way front paws move when a dog is excited would be heritable? But then, who expected that identical human twins who were raised apart would end up living in houses painted the same color, wearing unique rings on the same fingers and marrying spouses with the same name?

It's amazing what behavioral tics are heritable in dogs and people. The offspring of one of my Border Collies "talks" just like her mom, mouthing a list of vowels ("Aiy-ee-I-oh-you!") when excited. Two different people, at two different times, have commented that I work a jigsaw puzzle just like my mother. But it's not just trivial traits that are passed on from parents to offspring. Some heritable behavioral patterns make the difference between a happy dog owner or someone living in dog-owner hell.

A multitude of traits appear to run in family circles, from dog–dog aggression to possessiveness over their owner's lap to a tendency to redirect aggression to the owner. Inherited traits aren't all negative, by the way—sweet and docile natures are just as likely to be passed on from parent to offspring as problematic ones.

Of course it's not just genetics that influences behavior. Early development and learning play equally important roles. The dual importance of genes and environment hasn't always been understood. For years American behaviorists and European ethologists fought about "nature or nurture," arguing that one or the other played the most important role in shaping an animal's behavior. Fortunately for us and our dogs, that foolish argument has been over for decades, with all but the most radical acknowledging that behavior is a recipe in which the ingredients and the method of combining them are equally important.

A wonderful example of the interaction of genes and environment comes out of Stephen Suomi's laboratory at the National Institute of Health. Suomi, a primatologist who specializes in behavior, learned early on that the Rhesus macaque monkeys he studies are each born with their own unique personalities. Not only has he identified certain individuals (about 10 percent of the population) who are impulsive, a bit aggressive and generally less socially competent than others, he's found that these individuals exhibit these traits soon after birth. This kind of behavior is mediated by the amount of usable serotonin, a neurotransmitter, in the brain, and the amount of serotonin is partially a function of the genes the monkey inherits. So here we have individuals predisposed to get into trouble and to be aggressive when they don't need to be, driven by their genetically determined brain chemistry. What makes this especially interesting is that the environment in which each individual was raised had an important influence on to what degree this particular trait was expressed. A really good mom could overcome most of the effects of low-seratonin metabolism, while monkeys who didn't have wonder-moms were more influenced by their genetics. It's a perfect example of the blending of nature and nurture, and how genetics and environment both make big difference in how an animal behaves.

One of the encouraging implications of the dual importance of nature and nurture is that genetically mediated tendencies such as possessiveness and aggression can often be influenced by a solid knowledge of the "nurture" part of the equation. Applied animal behaviorists like me would be hard pressed to help many of our clients without a firm understanding of operant and classical conditioning. But as much as I love helping my clients, I'd rather help prevent serious and heart-breaking problems in the first place. If Kinko's owners had known a little more about the "like father like son" effect, and if the breeder had paid as much attention to disposition as she had to healthy hips, the owners wouldn't have been in my office, ashen-faced and exhausted, trying to decide whether or not to euthanize their four-footed best friend.

In spite of the significant influence of genetics on behavior, there is an unfortunate lack of awareness in this country of such an important, and in some senses, obvious fact. We all seem to "know" that behavior is strongly influenced by genetics—"a chip off the old block" and "the apple doesn't fall far from the tree" are well-worn folk wisdoms that reflect this understanding. The problem seems to be that we don't apply it when it's needed. If Kinko's owners had thought about it, they would never have taken a puppy from parents of such dubious dispositions.

And the breeder? I don't know the specifics in this case, but I could fill a concert hall with the number of "responsible" breeders who select for breed type, good structure and great coats and who carefully screen out heritable diseases…period. Time and time again, little attention is paid to the disposition of their breeding stock. I'm all for breeding for sound structure and good health, and I love a gorgeous dog as much as the next person, but, to add one more old-fashioned adage, "pretty is as pretty does."

Often, people who should know better focus exclusively on structure and physical health and ignore behavioral tendencies that can come back to bite them in future litters. In this case, I mean that literally. Our fascination with looks is so strong that it deserves its own essay (it seems that our focus on attractiveness is heritable as well!) and it's not always a bad thing. But we desperately need to reinforce breeders who do breed for good dispositions, and we need to educate dog owners to make choices based not just on looks and overall physical health, but also on behavior.

Last I heard, Kinko hasn't bitten since he visited my office, and his behavior to visitors is greatly improved. But his owners know they'll always have to manage him and that he'll never be quite the dog they wanted. Next time, they'll know not to be seduced by a handsome face. You can help prevent future Kinkos by passing on this essay to anyone you know who is about to breed a litter, or about to get a new dog. Heck, send it to anyone you know who's dating—wouldn't we all be better off if we paid more attention to behavior than to looks, regardless of the species?

AGGRESSION

Is it in the breeding?

I wish I hadn't seen the pictures. Although they were horrible enough. It was the look on her face. Alone in a hospital bed, nightgown pulled off to reveal the injuries, the 10-year-old-girl was being victimized yet again. First she was mauled by two dogs in her friend's front yard, now she was helpless and humiliated, violated this time by a police photographer recording her injuries.

It is the second case I've seen this year in which young children have been severely injured because their friends played fast and furious with their daddies' fighting dogs. The little girl above had angered her friend, who had blurted out "Get the meat!"—the cue she'd heard her father say to start the dogs fighting. It took 10 minutes to get the dogs off of the little girl.

I imagine that you might react as I did, disgusted by a father who would allow something like this to happen, by the mindless combination of his young, unknowing child and an animal he had exploited for his own amusement. It is easy to be shocked by the behavior of our own species. At times I am almost dumbstruck by the things that some people do with dogs. For example, I'm not sure that I want to meet the person who advertises his Caucasian Mountain Dogs as having "the knock-down power of a .45...with intelligence!" (I talked to a breeder of Great Pyrenees livestock guarding dogs once, who told me that his breed "was a loaded gun waiting to go off." I waited almost thirteen years for my sweet, gentle Great Pyrenees, Tulip, to "go off." Apparently she never got the memo.)

It is easy to find stories of stunningly irresponsible things that people say about dogs, that people do with dogs that get other people hurt, and that get individual dogs in big trouble. But that's too easy. That's about them. You know—"them," the people who don't read books like this. The people who don't raise, train or manage their dogs responsibly. "Them," as in "not us."

But I'm going to talk about us. Because even though two cases of fighting dogs turning on a child are more than enough, they are, thankfully, rare. But less dramatic cases, in which people get hurt or scared by dogs (cases that are not sensational enough to make the daily news in other words), are not as rare as you might think. What behaviorists see day in and day out is this: a dog who at eight weeks is growling/snarling over having his rawhide taken away. Or the dog who works himself into a frenzy of aggression during thunderstorms in spite of his owner's gentle attempts to manage him. Or a dog who growls, snaps and possibly bites when visitors enter the house. Or a dog who didn't want to get off the bed, and so bit up his owner's arm, crunching his way through her forearm, her elbow and her shoulder, until he finally attached himself to her ear.

Of course, because I specialize in working with canine aggression, it's not surprising that I see a litany of trouble. What's relevant to this essay is where the dogs come from, and who owns them. The answer is simple—they come from everywhere. From backyard breeders, from well-known show kennels, from humane societies, from champion field trial lines, you name it. They're mostly owned by nice, responsible people, many who have had dogs before and never had any trouble. In other words, they come from, and are owned by—*us*. Ouch. It's so much easier to focus on the dramatic horror stories, the huge, dangerous dogs owned by strange people, "other" people. It makes me squirm to write this; I can only imagine what it feels like to read it. But the fact remains that, although most of the 52 million dogs out there are remarkably polite, too many of them are too quick to use their teeth to solve a problem.

Barbara Woodhouse once said that "There are no bad dogs." Maybe not, but surely we'd all agree that some dogs are better than others. And some dogs are more likely to hurt people than others, and some of the traits that make them that way are inherited, as are physical traits like coat color and the shape of a dog's ears. I don't want to imply that breeding is the only factor in whether a dog might or might not be dangerous. It's not. Much of the aggression that we see has nothing to do with genetics. Much of it is clearly, and often tragically, explained by ignorant owners. Educating owners about how to humanely and effectively train a dog can have a profound effect on decreasing aggression. That's such an important topic that it deserves its own essay. But I'm going to put it on a "sit/stay" for now, because this essay is about genetics, and the importance of dog owners and dog breeders alike understanding how big a role good breeding can play in behavior.

There seem to be two extremes along the continuum of expectations that we humans have of our dogs—those dog lovers who don't know that training can solve myriad problems and those who believe that training can solve everything and anything. But as miraculous as good training is, it can't solve everything, anymore than the best coach in the world can make you a world-class basketball star. Learning and experience have to filter through the genetic blueprint that every dog starts with, and some dogs come equipped with designer plans for trouble. It's just a biological truth that there are some traits, many of them greatly affected by genetics, that can make a dog more likely to be aggressive than others.

One of those traits is shyness. Shyness is simply the fear of unfamiliar things, although it seems many of us like to avoid that word. "He's not really shy, he's just cautious of people he doesn't know." That would be, uh, shy. Shyness is highly heritable: You don't pass on a lot of genes in the wild if you continue the mindless curiosity of a young pup as an adult. Surprises usually aren't good if you live a life on the edge of survival. Of course shyness is also influenced by early environment, but because of individual differences, some dogs are at greater risk of developing into shy adults than others.

Like all the heritable traits that I'm going to talk about, shyness is not a yes/no trait, where a dog is either shy, or not. It's a continuum. And like all the other traits, it in itself doesn't cause dogs to bite. Some shy dogs hide behind their owners' legs all their lives. It's a combination of traits that creates dogs who hurt people. The shy dogs who get in trouble are also dogs who have what behaviorist William Campbell calls "active or passive" defense. "Passive" vs. "active" defense is the difference between the dog who stands and trembles when a stranger reaches out to pet her, and the dog who snaps at any hand near her head. Of course, sometimes both of those responses can be seen in the same dog, usually dependent upon her age and experience in life, but a dog's genetic complement is an important factor in how she's going to respond at any age.

Another trait that seems relevant is a dog's predisposition to use his mouth. It seems that all dogs don't come with an equal tendency to use their mouths to solve problems. For example, my Border Collie Pip apparently didn't read the chapter on Border Collies. Pip didn't work my sheep, because if they confronted her, she licked their noses and wagged her tail (right before she turned and ran away). It quite simply never occurred to her that she could use her mouth, not only to defend herself, but to get the sheep to respect her.

There are many other traits that seem to affect how likely it is for a dog to become aggressive to humans. I suspect that dogs who are what I call "status seeking" are much more likely to bite when you go to nudge them off the bed. Some dogs seem to have no frustration tolerance and lose their tempers when they don't get what they want. Some dogs are more "reactive" than others, alerting to the slightest stimulus and unable to recover from arousal after working themselves into a frenzy, while their brother is still yawning on the dog bed.

And let's face it: size matters. Take it from someone who has made a living for years working in a small room with dogs who bite people. Having a 10-pound dog bark and lunge at you is simply not the same as having a 90-pound dog do it, no matter what the breed. Some little dogs have huge teeth (ever looked in the mouth of a Jack Russell Terrier?), but the psychological impact of having a small dog go after you is simply not the same as having a big dog do it. Little dogs

may be able to hurt you, and very badly at that, but they're not going to bring you down to the ground. Want to be in the room with a
nervous, reactive, "active defense reflex," status-seeking, 120-pound
dog with no frustration tolerance? (Why is it that the phrase "the
knockdown power of a .45" comes to mind right now?)

The irony here, and the gist of this essay, is that we know a great deal
about the genetics of temperament in canids, but we're not using it
to our advantage. In a profoundly important experiment, a biolo-
gist name Belyaev began breeding Russian fur foxes for "docility."
He divided the foxes into three categories: those who bit or tried to
flee if you reached toward them with one hand while holding food
out with the other, those who stood immobile, and those who encouraged contact by licking the experimenter's hands, whining and
wagging with their tails. By breeding the foxes who solicited contact
with unfamiliar humans, he developed a line of foxes who not only
responded with docile greetings to strangers, they developed other characteristics of domestic dogs like piebald fur (think Springer
Spaniel or Border Collie), curled tails and changes in rates of development. Some of them even went into heat twice a year instead of
once a year, just like domestic dogs compared to wolves and Basenjis.
In just 30 generations he created what he called the "domesticated
elite," a line of foxes who enthusiastically licked the hands of strangers, rather than snapping at them.

But where is the blue ribbon for a docile dog? Exactly what social
support and rewards do breeders get for selecting for docile dogs?
Conformation shows select for, well conformation, and the ability
to "show well." Does "showing well" relate to being a good pet? Not
necessarily. Field trials for Retrievers select for drive and stamina,
dogs with a "never say die" attitude that doesn't always make them
the best addition to a suburban family. Of course it's not just determination that wins a dog a field trial title; a dog can't win without
being superbly trained. Obedience is important in field trials, as it
is in obedience trials and agility and herding competitions. But being able to learn to work as a team and to really listen to your team
leader during a performance is not the same thing as docility, or lack
of shyness or a lack of frustration tolerance. The only title that comes
close to testing for manners is the Canine Good Citizen award. It's a

fine effort in the right direction, and we need to acknowledge it and work on promoting and improving it. Exactly how much attention do well-mannered, polite dogs get? Is there a star-studded night of glitz and big money that celebrates them every year?

It is important to acknowledge here the many people who do pay careful attention to disposition. I know herding dog breeders who breed for useful working farm dogs who can nip a steer on the nose to load it into a truck, but who would turn inside out before they snapped at a child. I know conformation breeders who want to win Westminster but would never breed a dog they wouldn't trust when the UPS man came. I know many dog owners who spent months carefully researching the breed, the right breeder and the right puppy.

There are lots of wonderful breeders and buyers, there are just not enough of them, and they don't get enough credit. Truly good breeders do exist, who do their best, make the tough decisions, and keep making responsible decisions in spite of the pain and the cost, but they just don't receive much recognition. Some people even talk as if "breeding" were a dirty word, given all the dogs at shelters who need homes. But we know from research that those dogs are most often adolescents or older dogs, who had no responsible breeder to go back to when things didn't work out. Good, responsible breeders and well-educated puppy buyers can do much to keep dogs out of shelters in the first place.

So here's to you: to the people who know that breeding a dog least likely to hurt someone is more important than anything in the world. To the people who know that although training and conditioning can, and do, solve a myriad of problems, it is best to start at the beginning, with a sound set of genes that mean training is like paddling downstream instead of up it.

Aggression isn't simple, because behavior isn't simple. But what is simple is that we're not doing as much as we can to breed docile dogs. It's true that breeding for huge fighting dogs is terrifyingly wrong. But it's equally true that breeding and picking puppies without enough concern for friendliness is also wrong. This issue of dangerous dogs is not just about them. It's about us. Ouch.

TRAINING OUTSIDE THE BOX

Can you bet against your dog's nature and win?

How strong *are* a breed's behavioral predispositions, anyway? Can you teach a Spaniel to come on command even as a grouse huddles in a thicket directly in front of her? What are the chances of training a sheep-guarding Komodor to host a "welcome to the neighborhood" party for a bunch of unfamiliar dogs? In other words, how often, and how well, can training (or nurture) override genetics (or nature)? The answer? No one knows. At least, not until they try.

Of course, we can all make some pretty good guesses. Can you teach your Yorkie to back a bull into a truck? Probably not. Would your adolescent Border Collie be the perfect pet for an elderly disabled couple who live in the city? Okay. I take it back. We do know, sometimes.

But not all the time. Knowing the breed of a dog may allow us to make predictions about an individual's behavior, but I've met plenty of Labradors who wouldn't fetch, and plenty of Greyhounds who wouldn't run. Of course, in a generic sense, we do know enough about dog breeds to do a reasonably good job predicting an individual's size, shape and behavioral tendencies. That is, after all, what breeds are all about—breeds are merely subsets of all possible genetic combinations in the group of animals that we call dogs. Those possible genetic combinations *do* have boundaries, however, the broadest of which are established by the species we call *Canis lupus familiaris*.

We don't expect dogs to fly, live underwater or turn into butterflies because we all know that dogs are four-legged mammals who come looking and acting pretty much like Benji or Rin Tin Tin.

We also know that Spaniels tend to be especially interested in birds and small game, that Terriers love to dig and that Retrievers…well, you know. So the answer to the question on training overriding intrinsic behavior is both gloriously simple and intriguingly complicated. On the one hand, knowing an animal's genetic background allows us to establish probability, something like a weather prediction. "Seventy percent chance of rain showers today" doesn't tell you it's going to rain. It just says it's more likely to than not. Whether you take the prediction to heart and carry an umbrella to work depends on many factors: Has it rained every day for the last week? How much do you trust the prediction? And probably most importantly, what is the consequence if it does rain and you're unprepared? Are you going home right after work to walk the dogs, who couldn't care less what you look like? Or are you giving a keynote speech at a televised conference?

It's a similar process with the behavior of our dogs. Can your German Shorthaired Pointer be taught to come reliably every time you call while the two of you are walking in the woods? Well, it depends. His breed allows us to make our first prediction—GSP's were bred to work with a lot more independence than Retrievers or Border Collies, and it's no surprise to anyone that, in general, they are harder to train to come when called than a dog that was bred to work at your side.

However, even within a breed, individual dogs are not clones. Most GSPs quiver at the thought of chasing after a bevy of quail, but there are always a few who haven't read the breed description. That's true of individuals in every breed. Not all Greyhounds are passionate about running after a rabbit, and not all Border Collies obsessively herd the house cat. There is a tremendous amount of individual variation within a breed, and each individual's genetic inheritance creates behavioral predispositions that are stronger in some cases, weaker in others.

So far, we have two factors that allow us to make predictions about a dog's behavior—the first is his breed (or mix of breeds as best we can tell) as an indicator of a genetic predisposition to behave one way or another, and the second is his specific personality. Both play huge roles in every dog's behavior, and can tell us a lot about whether training can override an inherited tendency to find birds, herd livestock or dig up the backyard.

But a third factor must be considered when asking if a dog can be reliably trained to do any one particular thing. That factor is you. How much time do you have to devote to the exercise in question? How important is it to you? How good a trainer are you? The answers to these questions have to be balanced against who your dog is, what he wants to do and how much he wants to do it. Answering the questions honestly and objectively will go a long way to either getting the job done or avoiding frustration and failure.

Speaking of failure, there's one more essential factor that absolutely has to be added into the mix. What is the consequence of things not going according to plan? What if, in spite of extensive and expert training, your unleashed Italian Greyhound forgets herself and takes off after a rabbit?

Compare the consequences of your dog getting loose if you're in a small, fenced dog park to what might happen if you're walking next to a six-lane highway with cars going 75 miles an hour? Imagine the odds that your dog won't listen are the same in each case, say 5%. It's the same dog, with the same personality and the same amount of training. If you had to choose under which scenario to keep your dog on-leash, the choice most of us would make would be obvious, and it is solely and uniquely tied to the consequences of losing the bet.

I can tell you this: My Great Pyrenees, Tulip, was never off-leash when we went walking anywhere off the farm. Would it have been possible to teach her to reliably come when called even if a deer jumped up in front of us and dashed into the brush? You guessed it—I don't know. What I do know is that the probability of success was so low that it wasn't worth the risk, the time and the effort for me to find out. I knew the odds, which, because of her genetics, were heavily stacked against me. I had enough of a challenge keeping her from dashing across the road when going from the farmhouse to the barn.

On the other hand, I walk my Border Collies off-leash in huge expanses of open land, because in this case, genetics and training are on my side. I worked hard to teach them to come when called, I watch them carefully and don't let them get too far away from me. When they're adolescents, I even teach them that they'd better keep their eyes on me or I'll disappear myself. And, hey, let's be honest. They're Border Collies, the breed that is famous for being so easy to train. However, it's also true that the Border Collies I've had have varied tremendously in how easy they were to teach a 100 percent reliable recall. It took me over a year to teach Pippy Tay to come when called, first time, every time, even if a deer bolting from the brush in front of us. I don't believe I ever had to train Lassie to come at all—the reason, in actuality, that I named her Lassie in the first place. My Great Pryenees Tulip, bless her fluffy white soul, was a sheep-guarding dog, bred for centuries to work independently of people and to take charge of the situation on her own without waiting for a human back-up. She was also, well…Tulip, and very different from Bo Peep, my first Great Pyrenees, who was as content to stay with me or the sheep as Tulip was inspired to go cross-country.

As I write, I'm thinking that I should modify the answer at the beginning of this column. The next time someone asks me if training can override their dog's behavioral inheritance, I should say "I don't know—it depends." That in itself might not sound very helpful, but if you know what it depends *upon*—your dog's genetics, his personality, your level of training and commitment, and the consequence of failure—you'll have an answer that will serve you well.

Part Six

LAST WORDS

HOME IS WHERE THE HEART IS

Contentment is a complex matter

She came the night my husband said he was leaving me. A small, neat-footed little Border Collie, Lassie arrived late into a house gone silent. I leashed her to the bed beside me, and lay all night with my hand touching her soft back. Patrick lay in his own world, turned away from Lassie and me, across the great ocean of our king-size bed.

Lassie and I slept fitfully, reassuring one another throughout the night. In the morning I took her outside with the rest of the dogs. She stayed focused on me and my other dogs, so I let her off leash and allowed her to charge through the Wisconsin countryside after my own pack, who were delightedly dashing after some surprised small animal. I can't imagine what prompted me to try calling her name as she tore away from me, but I did. "Lassie," I called, "Lassie, Come!" It was absurd to think that a dog I'd barely met would be so responsive in that context, and I remember laughing at myself for even trying. Perhaps that's why I still have the image of her response in my mind—freeze frame of a small, black and white dog suspended in mid-air, twisting her front end back toward me, hindquarters still going away. She hit the ground running just as hard toward me as she had been running away and skidded to a stop at my feet, grinning like a cartoon dog.

I was just going to keep her for a few weeks. She was the daughter of my male dog Luke, and had been sold by the breeder to a woman who ended up single and in the city with three young kids. It was a good place for a Border Collie to go bad. If you don't like to come home, put on jeans and go outside in your football field-size yard for several hours, don't get a Border Collie. Smart, high-energy dogs who are bored always find something to do—it's just usually not what you want. True to form, Lassie drove her owner crazy by digging, barking and recycling the kids' toys. The owner loved her dearly, but she couldn't cope with Lassie's misbehavior, so she agreed to send her back to the breeder to give her another chance. I said I'd foster Lassie while the breeder was on her honeymoon. When she returned, she would take Lassie back, and we would both look for a good home for her.

That first morning Lassie seemed a bit restless, lying down and then getting up, never settling in one place for long. There was no question she was a bit anxious. But she was happy to play, slurped down her dinner with gusto and took to herding sheep like a professional. She slept soundly the second night, and by the third day you'd have thought she'd grown up here. I called the breeder and asked if we could skip the "finding her another home" part of our agreement. She's still here, thirteen years later, warming my feet as I write this.

Lassie's first owner decided not to keep her, and it was the most responsible and loving choice she could have made. Deciding to re-home a dog can be an agonizing process, and as an applied animal behaviorist and seminar speaker, I often encounter people who are suffering over what to do about a particular dog. Perhaps it's a bitch who has declared an all-out war on the other female dog in the house. Perhaps it's a dog who is marvelous with adult humans but is terrified of young children—and the owners are pregnant. Often it's a dog like Lassie—a square peg trying to pound herself into a round hole, and driving everyone crazy in the process.

There are many things that make re-homing a dog difficult. Besides the pure, slicing grief over an upcoming loss, there's a valid concern about finding the right home. I know it well. I remember sleepless nights when I thought about re-homing a Border Collie named

Scott, worrying obsessively that I'd choose the wrong place and end up sending him to some version of doggy hell. But there's another issue that comes up when good, responsible dog owners first think about re-homing a dog, and I think it's the hardest one to handle. We think of re-homing our dog as a Betrayal. I capitalized the word on purpose, because being betrayed is such a primal, pervasive fear that it can take on a life of its own.

What could be worse than selling your child? What act is more horrible than selling out a friend and then turning your back on him? Our society has strong feelings about family loyalty, and after all, you probably think of dogs as part of your family. All responsible, loving dog owners are appalled by, and painfully aware of, the real betrayals that people perpetrate on dogs. Dogs are beaten, starved, abandoned and tortured, and the rescuers among us are often overwhelmed with a desire to make up for such horrors.

But re-homing a dog whose needs you can't provide for isn't abusive, it's generous and kind. One of my clients rescued a herding dog from a shelter where she worked, but in just a few weeks he developed a severe aggression problem. After working with both of them for several sessions, it was clear to me that the dog could never adapt to life in a tiny city apartment. He was so tense in such close quarters that he could barely breathe. Even though his owner loved him deeply and was committed to solving his problems, her love, time and money couldn't make up for his soulful need for open spaces. He's doing beautifully now, out of the city, loose as a goose in a pack of slap-happy dogs, because his owner bravely accepted that her responsibility wasn't to hold on to him forever, but to figure out what he needed and find it for him.

All dogs need shelter and care and kindness, but beyond that, every dog is different. You might think that 13 acres in the country, a flock of sheep and an owner who's a kindly professional dog trainer would be the perfect home for any Border Collie, but it's not. My Border Collie Scott desperately needed to herd sheep for a living, not as a hobby, and he hated all the changes and excitement that happened on my farm. Scott moved to an isolated farm with hundreds of sheep who needed a serious, dedicated dog to work long hours every day.

I cried so hard when I drove away from his new home that I had to pull off the highway. But Scott adapted quickly to the life he'd always wanted, and within days both he and I were thrilled with his new home. Another of my dogs, Kit, herded sheep as if she were starting a billiards game—running straight at the flock until the sheep scattered, and then standing stock-still in the center, nonplussed about what to do next. Kit may have some of the best herding-dog genes in the country, but she had no more natural ability to herd sheep than you might have seen from a Bichon Frise. At the time, I desperately needed a herding dog, and it would have been unfair to put so much pressure onto a dog who showed no interest or natural ability in working sheep. Kit became the beloved house-dog and agility star of a dear friend of mine, and lived a life far better than she would have here.

In some cases, no amount of training, conditioning and skill can make up for an outside environment that clashes with the inside of a dog. That's why finding the right home for a dog whom you love doesn't have to be betrayal, and neither is it necessarily a failure. I lived in 12 places in eight years in my twenties, and I learned a lot from so much moving around. One of the things I learned was that it's a lot easier to be happy in some places than it is in others. I'm settled now, on my small farm in the hills of southern Wisconsin, and even after the most luscious of vacations, my heart swells when I come home to the rolling hills and woods of my little valley. I love visiting the vitality of busy cities, but I could never thrive in one for long. The mind boggles at the behavioral problems I'd develop if I were forced to live away from my beloved countryside. Lassie's behavioral problems shed off like a winter coat in spring after just a few weeks at the farm. I didn't have to re-train her or develop an elaborate treatment plan. Lassie's heart expanded into the open pastures around her, and within days she was as settled and calm as if she'd been here all her life. Home is indeed "where the heart is," but that doesn't mean you can toss your heart anywhere and be happy no matter where it lands. All of us, dogs and people both, need a place that allows us to be who we truly are, not who someone else wants us to be.

Of course, passing a dog around like a fruitcake can cause terrible harm. Most dogs will suffer if their homes shift underneath them like sand in the wind. It's important to know what your dog needs, and if it's clear that you can't provide it, then it's important to have the courage and the faith to find it for him. What each dog needs is different, and individual requirements must be carefully considered. There are many dogs, for example, who get worse—not better—in that fantasy "good home in the country."

It's an act of love, this scary project of finding fertile ground for your dog's soul. That's where your knowledge and skill are critical, just as when you carefully consider where to send your son or daughter off to college. It's a big responsibility to shoulder, it's true. But if it were truly necessary, you would no more be betraying your dog than you would be your child when you celebrate at her wedding. After all, we humans move from one family to another, eventually leaving our first home to fit into another one as we mature into adults.

Years ago, my husband Patrick left for good a few days after Lassie came, and for a time I thought my heart would break. But the bleakest of winters still lead to spring, and that sad season feels long ago and far away. Patrick and I are good friends now, and we are both happier than we've even been. He built a house just down the road. Tomorrow we will take the Border Collies on a walk—me with my dogs, and he with his dog Tess, the daughter of Lassie, who needed the love of her first owner to be able to finally come home.

Rites of Passage

Navigating the loss of a beloved dog

Tulip was as beautiful in death as she was in life. Her long white fur covered her old thin body like a fluffy blanket. Her eyes were peacefully closed, and she looked as though she might wake up at any moment and plunk her huge white head in my lap for petting.

Tulip died at the admirable age of 12 years, 10 months, a legendary length of life for a Great Pyrenees. But this not an essay about Tulip, although like many of our dogs, she deserves an entire Library of Congress written about her. Rather, it's an essay about coping with the death of our beloved dogs, and specifically, about how best to cope in the hours right after they die.

Here's my advice: If you can, spend some time with the body of your dog after he or she has died. (My mother called dying "going aloft," and I will forever be grateful for the way that lilting expression lightens up the subject.) Staying with the body may be hard for some people, and if it's too hard, then you shouldn't do it. Coping with death and dying is an exquisitely personal thing and it's impossible to say what's best for everyone. But, here's the thing: Staying with the body provides a transition between a house rich with the sound and action of a living dog and a home still and silent in their complete absence.

After she died, Tulip lay on the living room floor all night long. I don't know how many times I sat beside her and stroked her forehead, or lay down beside her and inhaled the rich scent of her fur. Tulip was there, but, of course, she wasn't there. What was left was a bridge for me to walk between *Tulip here* and *Tulip gone*. It wasn't easy; I don't need to tell the readers of this book how deep the pain can be when we lose a beloved dog. But it helped. It helped.

We forget, in our industrialized society, how important the ritual of preparing the body for burial used to be. Strangers didn't do it; the family provided that last loving act, a final way of paying respect and saying good-bye. And even though we no longer wash and wrap the bodies of our loved ones, we haven't forgotten the importance of the body to those who are still alive. Look at the lengths to which we go to recover the remains of a person lost at sea. Literally hundreds of thousands of dollars can be spent to bring just one body home to the family, and no one ever complains about the cost. We instinctively know how important it is to have physical contact with the body of a loved one. "Closure," we call it.

I wonder if dogs need closure too. I have kept the bodies of my deceased dogs overnight for my own sake, but also for the welfare of the other dogs in the house. I was motivated to do this by the stories of Andy Beck, a New Zealand horseman, who reports that mares who have been allowed to stay with the body of a dead foal cope better than mares who have not. I've had clients whose dogs waited at the window for the other dog to come home from the vet clinic—for weeks or months, and, in one case, years. Perhaps it *is* important for our pets to have closure too.

It's true that not all dogs behave as if they are paying respect to the bodies of their compatriots, much less that they understand something as complex as death. (Young children also have a hard time grasping the concept; they'll say things such as, "I know Daddy is dead, but when is he coming home?"). Some dogs seem to pay no attention whatsoever to the body of a former housemate, and the dogs who do may respond in a variety of ways. Many years ago, my dog Luke ignored his friend Misty's body all night until I prompted him to sniff her the next morning. I'll never forget the look in his eyes when he did—he reared back and looked straight into my eyes, his own eyes as round as pancakes. He seemed completely and utterly shocked. On the other hand, his niece, Pip, had circled Misty's body repeatedly right after her death, and then lay down beside it with a huge sigh. She lay there for hours and didn't leave for most of the night.

After Tulip died more recently, 14-year-old Lassie curled into a stiff ball, radiating anxiety and tension. She lay down beside Tulip's body and began to knead and suck on the blanket underneath her. Young Will, who's about 18 months, sniffed the body like a frightened horse. Leaning backward, ready to bolt, he inhaled deeply and noisily for several moments. Then he turned, found a toy and ignored Tulip for the rest of the night. I have no idea what was going through either of their heads, but still…it feels right to let the animals of the household see and examine the body of a deceased dog. It's hard to imagine it hurting anything, and it seems intuitively true that it might help.

We buried Tulip's body on a nearby knoll, where in life, she had barked away the coyotes that threatened the spring lambs, or rolled in the cool snow. We surrounded her body with the hundreds of tulips that our friends brought to the house the afternoon of her death. As visitors flowed in to celebrate her life, Tulip stood on her flagging back legs and soaked up their attention like a diva. We told stories of the day she almost died in a snowstorm, trapped under logs at the edge of a cliff. I recounted the day I first met her, when I explained to her breeders that she was the only female of the group whom I *would not* buy. Oh, she was the one who stole my heart—that was clear within the first five minutes—but she was also the one I couldn't take home because she was too active and playful to be a good sheep-guarding dog. I ended up with her anyway. Lucky me.

She's still here, I know, as much a part of the farm as the wild apple trees up the hill and the salmon-colored clouds at sunset. A few months after she died, the tulips we planted last fall splashed across the landscape, full of life and color. How sweet the sight of them.

PET PEEVES

Let's hear it for the family dog

"Just a pet." How many times have you heard someone say that? Perhaps it was a conformation breeder who observed, "This pup doesn't have a good top line, so he should be sold as *just a pet*." You've probably read the phrase in articles about how much we love our companion animals: "It is remarkable how much money the American public spends *just on pets*." And companion animal lovers use it—ask any veterinarian, who too often hears: "We just adore our little Cocker Spaniel, she's the greatest joy of our lives, but we can't afford to spay her because she's *just a pet*."

I like to think of myself as a reasonably patient person, but I find I'm losing patience with those three little words. I suppose it's because of what I do. I've spent almost 20 years working with people whose pet either brings them joy, relaxation and love, or anxiety, frustration and pain. Within the same day I might see a client whose dog prevented her child from walking across a busy highway, and another client whose dog mutilated someone's face. All this from the family pet—an individual who is looked upon with ambivalence by society at large. On the one hand, many of us afford our dogs a bounty of luxuries, as well as a kind of social and emotional intimacy usually reserved for members of the same family or, at least, the same species. On the other hand, pet dogs—companion dogs—have never been given the same level of import as working dogs.

Of course, part of this ambivalence stems from the inherent and obvious value of a working dog. Technology still can't replace a good herding dog, and there's not a machine in existence that can do a better job than a trained search dog of finding a buried bomb. However, the value of dogs who comfort our children and lighten our lives is less obvious. These dogs come without clear job descriptions, carrying metaphorical résumés that contain vague generalities with little inherent power. "Sweet, loving, with liquid eyes and soft fur. Great social skills. (Or not.) Easy to get along with. (Or not.) But worth it (see above: "sweet, loving, with liquid eyes and soft fur").

Perhaps part of our ambivalence stems from our conditioned response to the word "pet" itself. The word has been used in reference to companion animals only in recent times; it originally described "an indulged or spoiled child" (thus the derivation of the phrase "teacher's pet"). By the mid-16th century, it was used to describe orphaned, hand-reared lambs, and eventually was applied to any "little animal that was fondled and indulged."[1] Notice the words "spoiled," "fondled" and "indulged"—adjectives that do not inspire admiration, and certainly not words that engender our respect. No wonder many of us have started using the phrase "companion dog," aware as we are of some amorphous negative connotations of the word "pet."

I suspect there's another reason behind society's ambivalence toward companion dogs—our discomfort with the emotions they evoke. Emotions are private, primitive things, and sometimes we are better off keeping them to ourselves. An athlete isn't well served by walking toward a competitor with a grimace of fear on his face. Tears of frustration aren't going to move anyone up the corporate ladder. And yet, look what dogs do to us. They strip us bare and play with our deepest emotions, just as a Terrier shakes a rat. Dogs and people are connected not at the hip or even the heart, but at the limbic system, joined by the most primal part of our brains. Dogs make us vulnerable, pure and simple. That's fine with some of us, but it may make others uncomfortable and motivate them to downplay the importance of the family dog.

---

[1] From *Pets in America*, by Katherine C. Grier, a fascinating account of the history of pets in this country.

Thus, it's at least understandable that the value of companion dogs is often demeaned by society in general. However, people in the dog fancy itself are the ones who surprise me—people who love dogs and devote much of their lives to them. Surely it's this group, and I count myself as a member of it, who should be aware of the value of a dog in the heart of a family. We need to think of family dogs as the most important product of our breeding and training efforts. Consider what we ask of our companion dogs: to live with well-intentioned people who might know little about dogs or how to communicate with them, to put up with a variety of visitors with grace and good manners, to ignore most things of interest to a dog (dead squirrels and cow pies, for instance), and to keep their weapons safely sheathed behind their lips at all times.

I write this knowing the value of a good working dog as well as anyone. Last year, I made a judgment error and my ram ended up on the highway in front of my farm. If I hadn't had Lassie, 13 years old and still a brilliant herding dog, someone could have gotten killed. Sound, healthy puppies bound for the show ring are equally important—the knowledge and dedication required to produce quality cannot be discounted.

But we must never forget the role of the pet dog in our society, and acknowledge that there is little that is more important than breeding dogs who bring love and joy into a household. If anything, we should charge *more* for the "pet" puppies, for surely they have the most essential job of all.

Price of a well-bred pup with the potential to become a great cattle dog? $500 to $750.

Cost of a potential breed-ring champion?
$1,000 to $5,000.

Value of a companion dog who adds
joy and love to your home?

Priceless.

Suggested Reading and Viewing

The Alex Studies, Irene Pepperberg. 2002, Harvard University Pres.

Animals in Translation, Temple Grandin. 2005, Harcourt.

The Bark magazine, www.thebark.com.

Before and After Getting Your Puppy: The Positive Approach to Raising a Happy, Healthy and Well-Behaved Dog, Ian Dunbar. 2004, New World Library.

Canine Behavior Series: Body Postures and Evaluating Behavioral Health (DVD), Suzanne Hetts & Dan Estep. 2000, Animal Care Training.

Canine Body Language: A Photographic Guide, Brenda Aloff. 2005, Dogwise Publishing.

Don't Shoot the Dog, Karen Pryor. 1999, Bantam.

Excel-Erated Learning, Pamela Reid. 1996, James & Kenneth.

For the Love of a Dog, Patricia McConnell. 2007, Ballantine.

Great Dog Adoptions, Sue Sternberg. 2002, Latham Foundation.

How Dogs Think, Stanley Coren. 2005, Free Press.

How to Speak Dog, Stanley Coren. 2000, Fireside Books.

Merle's Door, Ted Kerasote. 2007, Harcourt/HCT.

The Other End of the Leash, Patricia McConnell. 2002, Ballantine.

Pack of Two: The Intricate Bond Between People and Dogs, Caroline Knapp. 1998, Delta/Dell Publishing.

Parenting Your Dog, Trish King. 2004, TFH.

Positive Perspectives 2: Know Your Dog. Train Your Dog, Pat Miller. 2008, Dogwise Publishing.

Raising Puppies and Kids Together, Pia Silvani & Lynn Eckhardt. 2005, TFH.

Social Pyschology, David Myers. 2005, McGraw-Hill.

The Truth About Dogs, Stephen Budiansky. 2001, Penguin.

About the Author

Patricia McConnell, Ph.D., CAAB is an Ethologist and Certified Applied Animal Behaviorist who has consulted with cat and dog lovers for over twenty years. She combines a thorough understanding of the science of behavior with years of practical, applied experience. Her nationally syndicated radio show, Wisconsin Public Radio's *Calling All Pets*, played in over 100 cities for fourteen years. She is the behavior columnist for *The Bark* magazine ("the New Yorker of Dog Magazines") and a Consulting Editor for the *Journal of Comparative Psychology*. She is Adjunct Associate Professor in Zoology at the University of Wisconsin-Madison, teaching "The Biology and Philosophy of Human/Animal Relationships." Dr. McConnell is a much sought after speaker and seminar presenter, speaking to training organizations, veterinary conferences, academic meetings and animal shelters around the world about dog and cat behavior, and on science-based and humane solutions to serious behavioral problems. She is the author of eleven books on training and behavioral problems, as well as the critically acclaimed books *The Other End of the Leash: Why We Do What We Do Around Dogs* and *For the Love of a Dog: Understanding Emotion in You and Your Best Friend*. For more information, go to www.patriciamcconnell.com or visit her blog, at www.theotherendoftheleash.com.